HOW TO ANALYZE PEOPLE WITH PSYCHOLOGY

11 Practical Techniques to Speed-Reading People Like the Experts. Learn Body Language, Facial Expression and Body Mirroring to Improve Your Empathy with Other People

JASON ART

Table of Contents

INTRODUCTION	7
Reading Clusters of Gestures Rather on Individuals	8
CHAPTER 1	
BODY LANGUAGES AND VOICE BASICS	13
Establish a Behavior Baseline	14
Look For a Cluster of Clues	15
Look at the Context, Setting, and Culture	16
Head and Face	17
Posture	20
Limbs	20
CHAPTER 2	
THE CLUE TO REVEALING TRUE INTENTIONS – EYES	22
How Does the Language of the Eyes Work?	23
So What Does This Mean in Terms of Non-Verbal Communication?	
	26
CHAPTER 3	
POSTURE AND ORIENTATION	28
Positive Body Language	28
Negative Personality Cues	31
Body Language and Posture	32
Proxemics	32
Eye Gaze	33
Touch	33
Appearance	34
Artifacts	35
CHAPTER 4	
NONVERBAL OF FEET AND LEGS	36
How to Analyze People through Nonverbal Behaviors of the Legs	36
Types of Leg and Feet Displays	37
Hand Display and Leg Display Combinations	39
CHAPTER 5	
NONVERBAL OF THE ARMS	41
How to Analyze People through Nonverbal Behavior of the Arms	41
Defensive Arm Displays	41
Arm Withdrawal	42
Arms Freeze Display	43

The Self-Hug	44
Territorial Arms Displays	44
Welcoming Arm Movements	45

CHAPTER 6
NONVERBAL OF THE HANDS AND FINGERS — 46

The hands and nonverbal communication	47
Active hand gestures	47
Hands are dangerous weapons	50
Waving	51
Raised hands	51
Handshaking	53

CHAPTER 7
NONVERBAL OF THE FACE — 55

How to Analyze People through the Nonverbal Behavior of the Face	55
What are Micro Expressions?	57
These micro-expressions are:	57
Facial Expressions can be faked!	59
Isolated Nonverbal Expressions	59

CHAPTER 8
HOW TO SPOT EMOTION WITH BODY LANGUAGE — 64

CHAPTER 9
HOW TO SPOT A LIE WITH BODY LANGUAGE — 69

The Psychology of Lying	69
Signs Someone Is Lying	70
Are They Telling Me the Truth?	72
Studying the Body Language of Liars	75
The art of recognizing sudden changes in Tone and voice	78
What to do to make lies obvious	79
When the Face Gives the Game Away	82
Spotting a Lie - The Most Common Gestures Used	84

CHAPTER 10
BEHAVIOR ANALYSIS — 88

Analyzing Social Behaviors	88
Behavior Is Largely Dictated By Selfish Altruism.	89
People Have Poor Memories.	91
People Are Emotional.	91

| People Are Lonely. | 92 |
| People Are Self-Absorbed. | 92 |

CHAPTER 11
COMMON PATTERNS OF INTERPRETING BEHAVIOR — 94

So What Exactly Is Behavior?	94
Actions Are Behavior.	94
Cognitions Are Behavior.	95
Emotions Are Behavior.	95
Everything Is Connected	96
#1 Establish a baseline	98
#2 Look for behavior deviations	98
#3 Start noticing a collection of gestures	99
#4 Compare and contrast	99
#5 Reflect	100
#6 identifying the resonant voice	100
#7 Observe how they walk	101
#8 Using action words	101
#9 look for personality clues	101

CHAPTER 12
READING PEOPLE THROUGH THEIR HANDWRITING — 103

Reading Letters of the Alphabet	103
Cursive Writing	105
Letter Size	106
Gaps between Text	107
Letter Shapes	107
Page Margin	107
Slant Writing	108
Writing Pressure	108
Signature	109
Stand Out Writing	110
Concluding	110

CHAPTER 13
WHAT IS BODY "MIRRORING"? — 112

CHAPTER 14
HOW TO USE "MIRRORING" TO IMPROVE YOUR EMPATHY — 119

| Why do we do it? | 119 |
| Copycat | 120 |

Getting the Girl	121
Beware of the Situation	122
Interviews	122
Crowd Pleasers	123

CHAPTER 15
HOW TO SPOT INSECURITY — 125

What clues or signs are evidenced by someone insecure? How can we identify him?	129
Factors Determining Good and Bad	130
Discovering Compassion	131
Identifying Someone with Insecurity	132
Insecure people try to make you feel insecure yourself.	133
Insecure people need to showcase his or her accomplishments.	133
People who are insecure drops the "humblebrag" far too much.	133
Insecure people frequently complain that things aren't good enough.	134
How to Spot a Dangerous Person	134

CHAPTER 16
HOW TO SHOW DOMINANCE THROUGH BODY LANGUAGE — 136

Appearing Larger	136
Make Your Body Appear Bigger	137
Stand Higher	137
Claiming Territory	138
Signaling Superiority	140
Show of Dominance through Wealth	140
Show of Dominance through Control	140
Controlling Time	141
Facial Expressions	142
Counteract Dominance	144
Return the Gaze	144
Initiate the First Touch	144
Take it Slow	144
Use Humor	145

CONCLUSION — 146

INTRODUCTION

Many people are inclined to the belief that understanding people and what they want is difficult. The fact that humans are capable of hiding their true intentions and thoughts supports this ideology, but only to a small degree. The truth is that human beings are the easiest to analyze due to the simple fact that we all tend to gravitate towards the same things.

In this book, we will go over some of the most powerful systems of personality analysis so that you can learn the skills that matter when it comes to mastering human psychology. With practice, you will be able to read people as the words on this page - and reap the benefits of having insight into people's thoughts and emotions. You will be able to improve your relationships and develop your powers of influence and persuasion by mastering this subtle but profound art of observation.

If you ask most people what they would like to achieve most in this life, the following answers will be prevalent:

- Money
- Career development
- Talent growth

- Happiness

- Prestige

- Peace etc.

We are all looking out for ourselves amidst a world with limited resources. The reason why you get up every day to work or study is all in an attempt to find your place in society and the world, and you must realize that everyone is in the same race. Therefore, before you attempt to study or analyze someone, you must keep the following factors in mind:

There are many factors to consider when assimilating signs from another person. However, two rules should be considered; cluster reading, which means gestures are analyzed in groups as opposed to being done separately. The other main factor is that the context must be considered too and not read in isolation.

Reading Clusters of Gestures Rather on Individuals

No-one is likely to be sending out singular signals because our brains are sophisticated enough to take in more than one clue consecutively. You might not even realize that you're doing it, but something does not ring true, so you start to look for as many signs that you can use to confirm or deny what you think is going on.

For example, when you think someone might be lying to you, don't just listen to what is coming out of their mouth but try to detect if their body language confirms or negates what they say. Below are a few suggestions that someone might be lying to you. In time, and with practice, you will be able to detect if someone is not telling the truth by knowing what signs to look for.

Looking up (trying to make up their story as they go along)

Covering their mouth (Can they believe what they are saying?)

Pauses (Don't know what to say next)

Blushing (I can't believe I said that, I'm sure they must know I'm lying)

It could be that someone uses something unique to them, but it is out of character, so it makes you sit up and notice. You then must draw on whatever other information is available to you.

A liar doesn't have to be lying maliciously either. It may well be that you ask a friend how they are, though they answer that they are feeling good, their body language tells you the exact opposite of what they've just told you. Look for corroborative evidence and never conclude on a clue, unless it's completely irrefutable. And even then, you might have misinterpreted it.

We are not usually consciously aware that we have so many clues coming at us to inform us about what is going on around us. But after being armed with this knowledge consciously, you can begin to look more closely for the clues and become more aware. The more you practice it, the more consciously you'll recognize the signs.

If you're trying to establish if someone is romantically interested in you and finally get them to go out for a drink with you, how does the evening progress? Are they mirroring your body language for instance? Which way are their feet pointing? If it's towards the door, then they're getting ready to run through it. Are they making eye contact with you? If not, they might be bored rigid. Are they laughing at your jokes? Or just smiling politely? Was that an eye roll? What more information do you need? Not everyone is going to think you're irresistible, even when you put your best foot forward, so you might as well cut your losses.

Unless, of course, you're confident you can turn things around and make them fall at your feet. Be honest with yourself. And face the facts. Write this one up as a practice or experience and move onto the next one. You're getting better and learning more each time.

Suppose you want to find out how your child's day has gone. How do you elicit more from them than 'fine' or 'okay'? Well, look at their body language and refuse to take what they are saying at face value. It helps if you can be casual about this and sit facing them so that you can mirror their body language and facial expressions. Try and present a relaxed stance and make sure your body language is open: open arms, uncrossed legs; make eye contact. If you do this, it helps them to feel that you're empathic instead of being judgmental. If you do persuade them to open up, try your best not to interrupt them. This is about them, not how you feel about it. If you start condemning them now, you might lose any future opportunity of discussion with your young person.

Only very rarely, do people say what they mean. It often needs more exploration that might be as simple as looking at their body language or noting it and following it up with a conversation. If you're alert, your relationships should improve in leaps and bounds.

Searching for Consistency

If you have ever observed a person taking a lie-detector test, you will realize that the interviewer always begins by asking questions such as:

Is your name Jane?

Are you Female?

Are you wearing a red shirt?

Is today Monday?

These questions are those that a person has no business lying, and they are used to identify the baseline i.e., how a person behaves when they are relaxed and telling the truth. Most employment interviewers also begin by asking similar questions, and it helps them establish the baseline of both verbal and non-verbal cues. That way, when they move into the more intense questions, they can be able to detect changes in demeanor.

When you meet any person you wish to analyze, you must be intent on getting the baseline from the word go. Regardless of whether you are meeting a person for a date or a potential working relationship, it is imperative to know their baseline actions. Otherwise, you will have a lot of trouble analyzing them.

This book is intended to help you gain a clearer perspective on your behaviors and patterns. This is something which can become tremendously useful insofar as helping you watch your gestures and mannerisms. This will allow you to convey the right message that you want to send to your interlocutors. You will not risk sending the wrong message, or mixed signals when you communicate with other folks.

So, let's get down to business. I am sure that you will find the information in this book to be useful and informative. You won't have to go searching for various books on the subject and combing through the Internet on websites that are littered with sales pitches and other gimmicks.

CHAPTER 1

BODY LANGUAGES AND VOICE BASICS

Do you know that people communicate much more through what they leave unspoken than what they say? Body language accounts for around 55 percent of the entire message during the process of communication. In a study conducted by Dr. Albert Mehrabian, it revealed that only 7 percent of our message is communicated through words, while 38 percent and 55 percent is conveyed through non-verbal elements such as vocal factors and body language, respectively.

"People are perpetually sending subconscious signals and clues while interacting"

Generally, what people say is well-thought and constructed within their conscious mind. This makes it easier to manipulate or fake words for creating the desired impression. Our body language, on the other hand, is guided by more involuntary movements of the subconscious mind. It is near impossible to fake subconsciously driven actions that we aren't even aware of. When you train yourself to look for non-verbal clues, you understand an individual's thoughts, feelings, actions, and more at a deeper, subconscious level. Try controlling the thoughts held within your subconscious mind and you'll know what I am saying.

People are perpetually sending subconscious signals and clues while interacting with us, a majority of which we miss because we are conditioned to focus on their words. Since primitive times, humans communicated through the power of gestures, symbols, expressions, and more in the absence of a coherent language. You have the power to influence and persuade people through the use of body language on a deeply subconscious level since it's so instinctive and reflex driven.

Here are some of the most powerful body language decoding secrets that will help you unlock hidden clues held in the subconscious mind, and read people more effectively.

Establish a Behavior Baseline

Create a baseline for understanding a person's behavior if you want to read him or her more effectively. This is especially true when you are meeting people for the first time, and want to guard against forming inaccurate conclusions about people's behavior. Establishing a baseline guards you against misreading people by making sweeping judgments about their personality, feelings, and behavior.

Establishing a baseline is nothing but determining the baseline personality of an individual based on which you can read the person more effectively rather than making generic readings based on body language. For instance, if a person is more active, fast-thinking, and impatient by nature, they will want to get a lot of things done quickly.

They may fidget with their hands or objects, tap their feet or appear restless. If you don't establish a baseline for their behavior, you may mistake their mental energy for nervousness or disinterest, since the clues are almost similar. You would mistakenly believe the person is anxious when he/she is hyperactive.

Observe and tune in to an individual completely to understand their baseline. This helps you examine both verbal and non-verbal clues in a context. How does a person generally react in the given situation? What is their fundamental personality? How do they communicate with other people? What type of words do they generally use? Are they essentially confident or unsure by nature?

When you know how they normally behave, you'll be able to catch a mismatch in their baseline and unusual behavior, which will make the reading even more effective.

Look For a Cluster of Clues

One of the biggest mistakes people make while analyzing others through non-verbal clues is looking for isolated or standalone clues instead of a bunch of clues. Your chances of reading a person accurately increase when you look at several clues that point to a single direction rather than making sweeping conclusions based on isolated clues. For instance, let us say you've read in a book about body language that people who resort to deception or aren't speaking the truth don't look a person directly in the eye.

However, it can also be a sign of being low on confidence or possessing low self-esteem. Similarly, a person may not be looking at your while speaking because he/she is directly facing discomfort causing sunlight. You ignore all other signs that point to the fact that the person is speaking the truth or is confident (a firm handshake, relaxed posture, etc.) and only choose to look at the single clue that he/she isn't maintaining eye contact to inaccurately conclude that the person is lying. Look for at least 3-4 clues to conclude. Don't make sporadic conclusions about how a person is thinking or feeling based on single clues.

For all, you know a person may be moving in another direction, not because they aren't interested in what you are speaking about or looking to escape, but because their seat is uncomfortable.

If you think the person is disinterested, look for other clues such as their expressions, gestures, eyes, and more to make more accurate conclusions. Include a wider number of nonverbal clues to make the analysis more accurate.

Look at the Context, Setting, and Culture

Some body language clues are universal – think, smile, or eye contact. These signals more or less mean the same across cultures. However, some non-verbal communication signals may have different connotations across diverse cultures.

For example, being gregarious and expressive is seen as common in

Italian culture. People speak loudly, animatedly gesticulate with their hands, and are generally more expressive.

However, someone from England may decipher this behavior as massively exaggerated or a sign of nervousness. Enthusiasm, delight, and excitement are expressed more subtly in England. For the Italian, this retrained behavior may signify disinterest. While the thumbs-up is a gesture of good luck in the west, in certain Middle Eastern cultures it is viewed as rude. If you are doing business with people from across the world, understanding cultural differences before reading people is vital.

Similarly, consider a setting before making sweeping conclusions through non-verbal signs such as body language. For example, a person may display drastically different behavior when he's at work among co-workers, at the bar, and during a job interview. The setting and atmosphere of a job interview may make an otherwise confident person nervous.

Head and Face

People are most likely experiencing a sense of discomfort when they raise or arch their eyebrows. The facial muscles also begin twitching when they are hiding something or lying. These are micro-expressions that are hard to manipulate since they happen in split seconds and are subconscious involuntary actions.

Maintaining eye contact can be a sign of both honesty and intimidation/aggression. On the other hand, constantly shifting your gaze can be a non-verbal clue of deceit.

The adage that one's eyes are a window into their soul is true. People who don't look into your eyes while speaking may not be very trustworthy. Similarly, a shifting gaze can indicate nervousness.

The human eye movements are closely linked with brain regions that perform specific functions. Hence, when we think (depending on what or how we are thinking), our eyes move in a clear direction. For example, when a person is asked for details that he/she is retrieving from memory, their eyes will move in the upper left direction. Similarly, when someone is constructing information (or making up stories) instead of recalling it from memory, their eyes will shift to the upper right direction. The exact opposite is true for left-handed folks. When people try to recall information from memory, their eyes shift to the upper left, whereas when they try to create facts, the eyes move towards the upper left corner. A person who is making fictitious sounds or talking about a conversation that didn't happen, their eyes will move to the lateral left.

When there's an inner dilemma or conflict, a person's eyes will dart towards their left collarbone. This is an indication of an inner dialogue when a person is stuck between two choices. Increased eye movement from one side to another can signal deception. Again, look for a cluster of clues rather than simply analyzing people based on their eye movements.

Expanded pupils or increased blinking is a huge sign of attraction, desire, and lust. A person may also display these clues when they are interested in what you are saying. If a person sizes you up by looking at you in an upward and downward direction, they are most likely considering your potential as a sexual mate or rival. Similarly, looking at a person from head to toe can also be a sign of intimidation or dominance.

When you are observing a person's face, learn to watch out for micro expressions that are a direct involuntary response based on feelings and thoughts. These reactions are so instinctive and happen in microseconds that they are impossible to fake. For example, when a person is lying, their mouth slants for a few microseconds, and the eyes slightly roll.

How can you tell apart a genuine smile from a fake one? Pay close attention to the region around the person's eyes. If someone is genuinely happy, their smile invariably reaches their eye and causes the skin around the eyes to crinkle slightly. There are folds around the corner of the person's eyes if they are genuinely happy. Another clear sign of a genuine smile is a crow's feet formation just under the person's eyes. A smile is often used by people to hide their true feelings and emotions. It is near impossible to fake a smile (which is so involuntary and subconscious driven).

Even the direction of a person's chin can reveal a lot about their thoughts or personality. If their chin is jutting out, he/she may be stubborn or obstinate about their stand.

Posture

When a person maintains an upright, well-aligned, and relaxed posture, he/she is most likely in control of their thoughts and feelings and is confident/self-assured. Their shoulders don't slouch awkwardly, and the overall posture doesn't sag. On the other hand, a sagging posture can be a sign of low self-esteem or confidence. It can also mean placing yourself below others or subconsciously begging for sympathy.

When a person occupies too much space physically by sitting with their legs apart or broadening their shoulders, they are establishing their dominance or power by occupying more physical space.

Limbs

Pay close attention to people's limb movements when you are reading them. When a person is bored, disinterested, and nervous, or frustrated, they will fidget with an object or their fingers. Crossing arms is a big signal of being, closed, suspicious, uninspired, or in disagreement with what you are saying. The person isn't receptive to what you are speaking about.

If you want to get the person to listen to what you are saying, open them up subconsciously first by changing the topic of conversation. Once they are in a more receptive state of mind, resume the topic.

When a person crosses their arms or legs, they are less likely to absorb or be persuaded by what you say.

A person's handshake can reveal a great deal about what they think about themselves or their equation with the other person. For instance, a weak handshake is a sign of nervousness, low self-esteem, and lack of confidence, submissiveness, and uncertainty. Similarly, a crushing handshake can be an indication of dominance or aggressiveness. A firm handshake implies self-confidence and a sense of self-assuredness.

Observe the direction in which a person's feet are pointed. If they are pointed in your direction, it means the person is interested in what you are saying. On the other hand, if they are pointed away from you, the person is looking for an escape route. Feet pointing in your direction or leaning slightly towards you are huge non-verbal signals of attraction.

CHAPTER 2

THE CLUE TO REVEALING TRUE INTENTIONS – EYES

The eyes are the windows to our soul—don't you agree? When we see a person for the first time, our gaze automatically goes to their eyes—looking, searching, and wondering who this person is.

In all honesty, it is easier to evaluate a person's heart than their mind. We can effortlessly pick up on our friend's mood or sense why our partner has dismissed plans to meet even without them speaking a word. How do we know this? How do we know what is going on in their heads without even speaking a word to them? For close friends, our partners, brothers, sisters, and family members—we just know simply because we grew up with them or because we've known them for a considerable amount of time to know what floats their boat, so to speak.

> *"In looking for clues in the eyes of a person, the first step is to know what that person is thinking"*

But how do we get this special access to the human mind towards acquaintances or your colleagues? Recent research tells us that looking at people's eyes is one of the ways to get in touch with the human mind, hence the phrase "I can see it in your eyes." It is poetic, and that's why you see it in so many music lyrics. While it's all beautiful and romantic, the truth is that the eyes can tell a lot about a person because while people can somehow hide their emotions and check their body language, they can't change the way their eyes behave.

How Does the Language of the Eyes Work?

When studying a person by looking in their eyes, firstly you need to do is subtly and not stare into their eyes. You need to maintain eye contact in a friendly manner and when you have established this, look into the changes in the pupil size.

A popular study published in 1960 says that the wideness or narrowness of pupils reflects how certain information is processed and how the viewer finds it relevant. The experiment was conducted by psychologists Polt and Hess from the University of Chicago, who analyzed both female and male participants when they looked at semi-nude images of both sexes. The study showed that female participants' pupil sizes increased in response when they viewed images of men and for the male participants, the pupil sizes increased when they viewed images of women.

Hess and Polt in subsequent studies also found that homosexual participants looking at semi-nude images of men (but not of women) also had larger pupils. This is no surprise at all because pupils also reflect how aroused we are. Women's pupils responded to images of mothers holding babies. This goes to show that pupil sizes do not reflect how aroused we are but also how we find a piece of information relevant and interesting.

This idea was brought forward by Daniel Kahneman who led a study in 1966. Kahneman is now a Nobel-prize winning psychologist. His study required participants to remember several three to seven-digit numbers and participants were to recall it back after two seconds. The longer the string of digits was, the larger their pupil sizes increased which also suggested that pupil size was also related to the information that the brain processing.

In looking for clues in the eyes of a person, the first step is to know what that person is thinking and to look deeply in their eyes.

Apart from the processing of crude information, our eyes can also send more sensitive signals that other people can pick up, especially if they are extremely intuitive. Another study conducted by David Lee began by showing participants images of other people's eyes and he asked them to determine what kind of emotions this person was experiencing. This researcher from the University of Colorado found that participants could correctly gauge the emotions whether it was anger or fear or sadness just by looking at the eyes.

he eyes also can reveal much more complex phenomena such as whether a person is telling the truth or if they are lying. For example, Andrea Webb conducted a study in 2009 which had one group of participants steal $20 from a secretary's purse and another control group was asked not to steal anything. This research led by The Webb and her colleagues from the University of Utah showed that pupil dilation gave away the thief. All participants were asked to deny the theft and the analysis of pupil dilation showed that participants who lied had pupils that were one larger by one millimeter compared to the pupils of participants who did not steal.

Our eyes also can become a good indicator of what people like. To learn to read the signs, you would need to look at the size of the pupil as well the direction of the gaze. Take for example someone choosing what they would like to eat at a restaurant. We are visual creatures anyway so our eyes are most likely darting between choosing the salad or the cheeseburger.

The other point to look into his decision making. When we are making a difficult decision, our eyes tend to switch back and forth between the different options in front of us and our gaze ends at the option that we have chosen. By observing these little details of where someone is looking, we can identify which options they choose.

Another way of studying this type of difficult trade-off is by offering monetary bets to participants. A study conducted at Brown University by James Cavanagh was when participants were asked questions that involved difficult tradeoffs between probabilities and payoffs.

Participants were paid based on their decisions. The researchers were kind that the harder the decisions were, the more the pupils of the participants dilated. As the choices got harder, our pupils also got bigger.

The eyes also give away clues as to if we experienced something unpleasant. Another study on eyes and their reaction was conducted at the University of Washington in 1999. The painful stimulation was administered to the fingers of 20 participants and they were asked to rate this pain from tolerable to intolerable. The more intolerable the circumstances were, the larger the pupils of the participants became.

Although pain is a very different feeling than looking at images of seminude people, it still showed a change in pupil response. This shows that pupil size correlated with the strength of feelings and whether those feelings were positive or negative. So if you want to know whether a person is feeling bad or good, consider the context and look into their eyes.

So What Does This Mean in Terms of Non-Verbal Communication?

Can we read everything just by looking at the eyes? Are the eyes the only signals we should concentrate on?

The thing is, the eyes are just one of the indicators or signals that we communicate with. When making high-stakes decisions duh as whether a person is guilty of a crime, pupil dilation is not something you solely rely on to make a judgment.

We should also look into context. That said, we are more perceptive to the body language of the people we always come into contact with compared to total strangers simply because we can tell their regular facial expressions apart from the non-regular ones.

To make better assessments of feelings, we need to look at various other evidence or elements of body language and course context. Because people cannot change how their pupils behave, the eyes are often used as a source of information to help create a better relationship simply because it enables us to empathize better. You may not be able to read a person's exact thoughts just by looking at their eyes but it still is a good perspective to study body language and read people.

CHAPTER 3

POSTURE AND ORIENTATION

The same way you train a dog to listen to your body language and cues, you can train a human being to follow you without question. The first step to control those around you lies in analyzing them, however, which is why this will discuss how to analyze people based on their body language.

Positive Body Language

"The most important asset anyone has is their smile"

There is a chance that you or someone you are observing is feeling insecure and trying to mask it. However, if you are not dealing with the melancholic personality, you might be dealing with a choleric personality. Everyone has heard the phrase "Fake it until you make it." This is the dogma of the choleric personality type. Whether they were cut out for something or not, they will not give up easily.

If you are confronting this type of personality, simply the mere act of uncrossing your arms or legs should gain you a little confidence. Add to that a genuine smile for the next person that you encounter and watch as they lighten up a bit in response. It might take a little practice, but this type of body language gives you control of the situation.

Understanding eye contact: This one can be tricky as it is easy to misinterpret but long eye contact is almost always meaningful in some way shape or form. If a person can look at you without looking away for more than a few seconds, then usually they are confident around you and are likely to be genuine. This is likely to be your phlegmatic personality type; one who is displaying a little bit of awkward shyness. They will notice you scanning the room, but do not count on them calling you out on this.

Typically, eye contact can make you look interested and says a lot about the person you are dealing with. If you find yourself being stared at by a person, you are likely dealing with a sanguine personality. This personality type is an observer and tends to be the sincerest of the four. By looking people in the eye, it is their way of proving those qualities.

Depending on the situation, you can look down and away out of shyness. When people are shy, they are deemed innocent. Your phlegmatic personalities are good at this as well. You want to seem innocent, no matter what your intentions as the best choice for drawing other people in are to keep them interested. Since you want people to trust you, you have to get close enough to analyze what type of personality you are dealing with.

If the other party looks away and down, and then back up at you, take advantage of this opportunity to consider them more closely. This is a sign of vulnerability which means they trust you, so you are free to do with that trust what you may. This is often a good time to ask them about themselves or offer something personal to break the ice. Compliments are always a good choice as it is hard to dislike someone who has recently played you a compliment.

Smile: The most important asset anyone has is their smile. A smile is a window to the soul. If you are walking down the street and someone gives you a genuine smile, it can change your day. That is the power you want to carry around with you. This is the gift of most sanguine personality types. They are cheerful on the outside and can easily make people laugh. Faking a smile is hard. The truth of any smile lies in the eyes. Pay careful attention to the lines that form when the cheeks rise as the evidence of a genuine smile forms.

If you ask someone to do something and they decline, smile anyway, they will feel bad for saying no. Depending on their actual reaction, say it again in a different way and a cartoonish voice (humor), and follow up with a serious voice. Ask for the favor again by adding another smile. This is best used in social situations and is to be avoided at work. Unless you are super cool with your co-workers or if you are sure you are dealing with a sanguine personality.

If your co-worker or your boss display a dislike for emotions or seem impatient, you could be dealing with a choleric personality. You will need to make it seem like they are the leaders. You're pushing boundaries, but you don't want anyone to recognize this game. No matter how it ends, do not give too much of a reaction. If you are too happy, it could kill the vibe. The same is true if you are too upset, just smile. You will not be able to change your personality type as the theory is that you were born that way. However, knowing more about yourself, you can control the display, or even master your weaknesses to have influence or get close enough to other people, that you may sincerely analyze them.

Negative Personality Cues

Now that you have a basic understanding of positive body language, let us look at the opportunity to dig into the negative cues often given by different personality types. Sometimes even the most trustworthy and genuine people can give off signals of distress through body cues, so it is important to take them with a grain of salt to avoid being misled.

If you find someone who is trying to discourage you, or they are judging you, their personality is likely phlegmatic if the negativity you are picking up on is coming from someone who is demanding attention or seems phony; you are amidst a sanguine personality type. You want to know the difference and how to respond to either situation to achieve a goal. Whether it is to cheer someone up, so you can enjoy their company, or perhaps you need to get away from someone who would seek to destroy your aura. Either way, practice makes perfect, and observing takes a lot of it.

Personal space: If someone moves away from you, this is often a sign that they believe you either did something wrong or you represent something negative to them.

This mentality applies to all four of the personality types. It hurts to feel rejected. Instead of feeling sorry for yourself, move back into their realm if you want to change the vibe.

Body Language and Posture

Posture and general movement might also express a big deal of information. A study on body language has developed considerably since prehistoric days; however, well-known media have concentrated on the over-interpretation of protective postures, arm, and leg crossing. Whereas these nonverbal acts can show thoughts and attitudes, the study indicates that body language is far more restrained and less perfect than formerly believed.

Proxemics

Individuals often refer to the need for personal space which is as well a vital style of nonverbal communication. The level of space people needs and the level of space people tend to perceive as belonging to them are swayed by several factors comprising social models, intellectual potential, situational aspects, personality distinctiveness, and level of knowledge. For instance, the amount of individual space required when having an informal talk with another person frequently varies from one to four feet. On the contrary, the individual distance required when talking to a group of people is approximately eight to twelve feet.

Eye Gaze

The human eyes play an important role in nonverbal communication and such aspects as staring looking and blinking are considered significant nonverbal acts.

When people meet someone or things that they adore, the pace of blinking goes up and pupils enlarge. On the other hand, staring at another individual may show a variety of emotions comprising hostility, concern, and desirability.

People as well use eye gaze as a way to conclude if someone is being sincere. Usual, fixed eye contact is frequently taken as an indication that someone is telling the reality and is dependable. Deceitful eyes and failure to keep eye contact, on the contrary, is often perceived as a pointer that somebody is dishonest or being misleading.

Touch

Communicating by use of touch is another essential nonverbal conduct. There have been considerable amounts of study on the significance of touch in childhood and infancy. For instance, a baby raised by a negligent mother experiences lasting deficits in conduct and social relations. Touch generally might be used to communicate love, awareness, compassion, and other related emotions.

On the other hand, touch is similarly used as a technique to communicate both position and authority. Researchers have established that high-status persons tend to attack other people's individual space with superior rate and strength than lower-status persons. Gender differences as well play a part in how individuals use touch to bring out the intended meaning.

Appearance

People's preference for color, outfits, hairstyles, and other aspects affecting appearance is regarded as nonverbal communication. Research has confirmed that diverse colors might suggest different personal moods. Besides, appearance might also change physiological responses, judgments, and understanding. For instance, just imagine all the restrained decision people rapidly make about somebody based on their look. These initial impressions are vital, and that is why specialists propose that work seekers dress decently for interviews with likely employers.

Researchers have also established that appearance might play a part in how individuals are viewed and how much money they make. For example, a study carried out on attorneys established that attorneys perceived as more attractive than their workmates earned practically more than those viewed as less good-looking. Culture is a significant sway on how appearances are viewed. While slenderness is respected in Western cultures, some African cultures associate full-figured people with superior health, prosperity, and social class.

Artifacts

Items and images are as well as tools that might be deployed to communicate nonverbally. In an online discussion, for instance, people may pick avatars to symbolize their distinctiveness, and converse information on who they are, and the things they adore. People frequently spend time creating a particular picture and surrounding themselves with items planned to transmit information regarding the things that are vital to them. Uniforms, for instance, may be applied to share an amount of information regarding an individual. A warrior shall put on fatigues, a police force will dress in uniform, and a physician shall dress in a white lab coat. From a bigger perspective, a simple glance at this attire tells everybody what an individual does as an occupation

CHAPTER 4

NONVERBAL OF FEET AND LEGS

We naturally spend so much time observing all nonverbal communication above the waist that we often overlook the importance of the legs and feet in body language. Both have a lot to say, and, when combined with the other parts of the body, can be used expertly to understand and predict behavior.

"our subconscious or true feelings are presented through them"

How to Analyze People through Nonverbal Behaviors of the Legs

When analyzing the body language of the legs and feet, it is essential to recognize why internal feelings and thoughts manifest through them. Hand gestures are seen naturally as a communicative medium. It is because we write words with them, paint with them, clap or shoo away someone with them - they are inherently understood on a human level as being used for communication. We do not think about the legs and feet in the same way. They are for walking, kicking, and jumping - so why should we pay attention to them?

It is precisely because we overlook the legs and feet that we should pay attention to them. When trying to psychologically control our speech, hand gestures, trunk posture, facial expressions, and eye gestures, we put so many cognitive resources towards them that we forget ourselves about our legs and feet as ways to communicate. That makes them pretty unique. It means that our subconscious or true feelings are presented through them for the most part rather than deception.

That is a powerful thing to know when analyzing behavior. With that knowledge, you can decode a person's thoughts through how they use their legs and feet. To do so, pay attention to:

- Gait or stance

- Feet position

- Crossing or locking of legs and ankles

- Fidgeting feet and leg movement

Types of Leg and Feet Displays

There are several ways in which we display our legs and feet, subconsciously (and occasionally consciously) conveying our internal psychology through them. Some of the most important ones to look out for are:

Leg Crossing: Both men and women cross their legs. It can be similar to when the arms are crossed, protecting vulnerable parts of the body and being closed off. It is especially important when interpreting possible sexual thoughts. However, the most critical component is not the way the legs are crossed, but rather where they are pointing. When someone crosses their legs, but the legs or feet naturally point towards a person that conveys the opposite feeling - this is an open gesture, which means a person is willing to listen.

Ankle Crossing: When the feet cross over each other, and the arms are crossed, this "locking" posture is usually defensive. However, when the ankles are crossed, and the legs are splayed, this conveys a relaxed state.

Leg Splaying: Speaking of leg splaying, if crossed legs can imply a closed-off attitude when the legs are either parted widely (most commonly in men) or straightened out in a Y position when sitting, this conveys relaxation. However, it can also display a lack of care for how others perceive the person doing the leg splaying, which can imply recklessness. This takes up unnecessary space and can also be seen as an aggressive territorial claim.

Shaking or Wiggling: An extremely common stress adapter is leg shaking or feet wiggling. Many people are unaware they are even doing it. It implies anxiety of some kind, with the movements taking the mind away from those thoughts and calming the limbic system. It can also suggest irritation.

Foot Tapping: Subtly different from foot wiggling, the rhythmic tapping of the foot can, of course, simply mean someone is enjoying the pulse of the music. However, it can also mean that a person is feeling impatient and anxious to get moving.

Stride: Most feet and leg displays involve sitting down, but a pace while walking can tell us a lot about someone's state of mind. If the stride is stable and not overly hurried, then the person is feeling confident. If the pace is erratic and uncertain, then there is anxiety there, most probably some sort of social worry about how others perceive the walker.

Defensive Leg Displays: Keeping the knees clamped tightly together can be a dead giveaway that a person is feeling defensive. Of course, it can also be because a person is wearing a skirt, so always be mindful of how the context affects interpretation.

Hand Display and Leg Display Combinations

It is essential to be aware of specific hand displays that can be combined with leg displays, altering their meaning. It usually involves the touching of the legs in some way. When we talked about adapters, we mentioned hand cleansing, which is when a person rubs their hands on their thighs. It can alter how we perceive the leg position. For example, one ankle may be resting on the other thigh, creating an open, relaxed stance. However, when hand cleansing is introduced, this shows that there is some anxiety and that the leg position is only part of the picture. Likewise, someone could be sitting looking relaxed with their arms by their sides, but the legs are tightly crossed. Again, this gives us something to ponder. We must then look for other non-verbal cues that would allow us to weigh the two behaviors, giving us a better chance to figure out which one is most prevalent and current in the person's mind. Any self-touching of the legs can be interpreted as representing anxiety, even knee clasping when both hands are clasping one or both knees.

CHAPTER 5

NONVERBAL OF THE ARMS

Now that we understand the basics of where nonverbal communication comes from, its place alongside verbal communication, and how to analyze a person's body language, etc., we can now learn about specific gestures, postures, and expressions. These will help you predict and understand a person's thoughts and goals.

How to Analyze People through Nonverbal Behavior of the Arms
The arms always depict some sort of nonverbal internal emotion or thought. It manifests as either a posture or a gesture. When analyzing the position of the arms, look for how the arms are held almost

> *"The arms always depict some sort of nonverbal internal emotion or thought"*

still. It could be in an open stance (arms extended out welcomingly) or a closed posture (arms folded defensively). When you analyze the gestures, look for how the arms move around.

Defensive Arm Displays

We have used the example of the arms folded in front of the body several times so far, and this is because it is one of the most common postures in nonverbal body language. It's also often one of the easiest to interpret. As we mentioned earlier, the arms are crossed in front of the stomach, which is a vulnerable area due to only being partially protected by the rib cage. It then is often seen as a protective stance. It is exhibited usually for one or more of the following reasons:

Feeling defensive at what is being accused or said. It could merely be disagreeing with the content of a significant other's speech.

Feeling nervous or anxious. By crossing the arms, not only is a person protecting themselves, but they are also trying to hide and not be noticed.

The person is feeling comfortable, and folding their arms is the most comfortable position for them to take at that time.

Notice how the last point disagrees with the first two. You must look for other nonverbal signs to either support or refute your initial interpretation. An example would be if the person were sitting down and locking their ankles together or crossing their feet. It is commonly seen with folded arms and is highly correlated with a defensive or negative attitude. Lastly, look for what the hands are doing alongside the folded arms. If they are clenched, this represents even more tension in the body and their attitude.

Arm Withdrawal

If you notice a person's arms being pulled inward towards their body, this can mean that they disagree with what you are saying, or even with who you are as a person. It can also convey disgust and anger. It can also represent apathy and a desire to withdraw from a conversation or situation. This movement can be significant, but it can also be subtle. Keep an eye out for anyone withdrawing their arms towards their body even slightly.

Arm withdrawal is often presented alongside leaning away from the speaker, facing away from them, or disgusted and bored postures and facial expressions. In some instances, the offending person does not even need to speak to cause this defensive behavior.

Arms Freeze Display

We naturally communicate with our arms and hands. These are among the most common gestures, and so movement in the arms is a continual way of communication. However, in some specific circumstances, these movements can halt. The arms become entirely still, often staying lifeless at the side of the body, but they can also freeze into other postures. This "Arm Freezing", is usually a sign that something is amiss. Remember earlier, we talked about the fight, flight, and freeze response? Arm freezing is the product of the freeze component. We tend to stay very still naturally when we believe there is a threat nearby. It is a way to avoid detection by dangerous human beings or animals. In this sense, then, arm freezing is usually a bad sign that a person doesn't just feel defensive, but that they feel threatened.

If someone presents this behavior, it could mean that they are overwhelmed with stress or that they feel ideologically or personally threatened by something or someone nearby. It is essential to recognize this behavior and try to set the person at ease if their arm freezing seems disproportionate.

The Self-Hug

How we have certain nonverbal behaviors which are designed to calm or vent a painful internal emotion? A self-hug is an excellent example of this. It can be seen when a person wraps their arms around the front of their body and then holds the outside of the opposite arm. There can sometimes be a rubbing or hugging motion as well. It is an adapter to make a person feel better if they are stressed. The stress can be slight or more pronounced.

We often naturally use this posture when preparing for a difficult situation like hearing bad news or waiting to face an exam. Caution should be taken; however, self-hugging can also mean a person is cold. Again, look for other nonverbal and verbal signs which will help you decide this behavior.

Territorial Arms Displays

The arms can be used to mark off territory. It can be a space or even a person. It is common to see partners with their arms around each other or arms locked together in public places. While this can be purely affectionate, it can also be a way to say to others, "this is my mate." Of course, we do not like to think of people as objects, but we have to remember how impulsive our brains can be. We are, after all, part ape, and those brain impulses are still competing alongside our humanity and even-mindedness. An example of this would be seeing your partner talking to someone attractive and then walking up and smiling while putting your arm around your partner. It is a definitive territorial behavior.

When marking off territory with the arms, you may also see people stretch out or lean against something with their arm or elbow. It is a way to say "this is mine." You might also see yawning used as an adapter in some situations, allowing a person to stretch their arms out around them. We accept that someone might stretch for comfort while yawning, but it is also often used to establish personal space. Moving the arms around, you can also mean that you want to be isolated and left alone.

Welcoming Arm Movements

We have focused heavily on adverse arm movements and postures, but the arms can also be used to say positive things. When arms are outstretched in front of a person, especially in a Y formation, this represents a hugging motion. Likewise, when a person opens up their body during conversation and the arms part to show their torso, this is a sign that they are responding to what is being said and welcoming of it. It can also be a sign of developing trust.

CHAPTER 6

NONVERBAL OF THE HANDS AND FINGERS

Hands and fingers are extensions of the arms but their association with communication is more commonly recognized by more people. A large part of this has to do with the fact that often we actively use our hands and fingers to communicate with other people. We use our hands and fingers to tell other people to stop or proceed, to encourage them or dissuade them, to signal peace or encourage confrontation, and a host of other gestures meant to say something.

> *"they were a communication tool among the many functions that they had and still have"*

The hands and fingers still send messages to other people when we are not aware. These are called passive nonverbal cues and they speak just as loudly as the passive gesture.

Both of these types of nonverbal uses depicted by the hands and fingers - active and passive nonverbal cues - are both important and we will explore the roles of these types of cues related to these parts of the body.

The hands and nonverbal communication

Hands and fingers play a huge role in the communication process. So much so that a whole system of communication has been developed around using them to communicate and this is called sign language. Sign language is the communication whereby a person uses hand and finger motions to substitute verbal communication. Sign language uses active hand and finger gestures. Active in this sense speaks to the fact that a person wants to communicate a certain message and therefore, deliberately uses a signal that sends this message.

Active hand gestures

Human beings did not start out using verbal communication as the primary way of expressing thoughts, feelings, and opinions. While the mouth was able to express grunts and other sounds, the range was not wide enough to allow our cavemen ancestors the ability to express all that they needed to survive. The hands were the saving grace in that time and thus, they were a communication tool among the many functions that they had and still have.

The use of the hands as a communication device has stuck with us through human evolution even though verbal communication has developed exponentially. Even verbal communication would not be as enriching as it is now without the use of the hands to enhance what is being said. Hands are the nonverbal complement to what is being verbally communicated and so, our brains have become hardwired through the evolution of our species to seek out what the hands have to say to complement what is being said or to contradict it. This is why we often pay so much attention to what the hands say. The brain is programmed to give the hands a great amount of attention when we read the messages someone else sends while we communicate, unlike the relative lack of attention it normally pays to feet and legs. The level of importance that we give to the hands when it comes to communication only comes second to the importance that we place on facial expression as a nonverbal communication device. The hands give solid hints as to what is happening to a person mentally and emotionally because more neural connections exist between the brain and hands compared to any other part of the body.

Not everyone is adept at interpreting the message that the hands send though even though we are hardwired to notice them during the communication process. Some people are better at reading hands compared to others. There is a scientific research that shows toddlers who use more hand gestures at that stage in their life have greater language abilities, and cognitive intelligence later on in their life.

The link between the hands and communication may be that not only is it relatively close to the brain, but also because the sense of touch grounds us to our parents and caretakers as babies. Touch is commonly done through the hands, and so we look for that touch from that moment.

The functions that the hands have when it comes to communication include:

- Substituting words. An example of this is holding up the hand to indicate that a person should stop rather than using the word itself.

- To support verbal communication with an illustration. For example, you can show a person how high you mean when you are talking about height by holding your hand up to the appropriate height.

- To give directions. A person may point to show where they are talking about even if they do not use cardinal points and direction-indicative words like north or south.

- To give a visual representation to support the verbal dialogue. For example, when talking about shape, you may use your hand to depict a circle or a square.

- To simplify complicated explanations. Sometimes the use of specific jargon or big words can make an explanation hard to understand but the use of gestures can support those items and make them simpler to understand.

Hand gestures and verbal communication go hand in hand so well that we most often move our hands in time to the message we are sending verbally.

Some hand gestures are easier to interpret in meaning compared to others and these are normally active gestures. Let's take a look at common active hand gestures now.

Hands are dangerous weapons

Before the invention of guns and even knives, humans had to defend themselves from different threats from other human beings, animals, plants, and more. Human beings had to defend themselves from these attacks and more, and therefore the most instinctive and ready weapons were hands.

There are a variety of ways that the hands can be used as weapons whether a person is on the offensive or defensive such as curling the fingers to form a fist, and pointing the fingers to form a shape resembling a spear.

Getting the point across that the hand can be used as a weapon does not mean that a person has to use it as such. Just forming a fist or other weapon look-alike can show another person that this person intends to or will use their hands in such a manner.

"I mean no harm"

As opposed to using the hands as a weapon, they can be used as a sign of peace and allegiance. This signal is done by opening the palms of the hand. The gesture can be done to show the other person that his person is not armed and is therefore not a threat. It is similar to a dog showing its throat to another as a gesture of submission or surrender.

Open palms are also linked to truth and honesty and this is why placing an open palm over the heart is done while making oaths in the courtroom. The gesture is performed by holding one or both palms open.

Opening the palm can also be a sign of apology or that a person did not mean to upset another.

Because this is a universal sign of truth, some people will deliberately use it as a way to deceive others. Therefore, you need to look out for contradicting body language if you ever suspect that person is lying to you while using this hand gesture.

Waving

This is a common active hand gesture that is often used as a greeting.

Despite the mostly positive connotation of this gesture, it can be negatively interpreted if not combined with positive body language. For example, if the wave is done with the back of the hand facing the other person, this can be seen as a dismissive gesture and thus, insult the other person.

Raised hands

Because the hands are such a powerful tool used in communication, a raised hand has been seen as a sign of authority or power over others for thousands of years. This gesture was so significant that all the people of power or authority had to do was simply raise their hand to signal that they had the floor and so, no one else was allowed to speak or interrupt during that time. This gesture dates back so far that persons of lower social status were executed for interrupting Julius Caesar in Roman history.

We live in a vastly different time and era now, but the raised hand still holds significance when used in social settings. Just look at the Italian and French cultures and you will notice that they are one of the societies that still place great significance on hand talking. In the Italian culture, taking a turn to talk in a group setting (even a group of just two) is a simple matter of raising your hand to signal that you want the floor. As a sign of respect to the talker, listeners will place their hands down or behind their back to show that they have recognized the symbol and are granting this person's request to hold the floor at that particular time.

The only trick is to get your hand up as fast as possible when you would like the floor to get a word in. Don't worry, this is not that difficult. It is a simple matter of looking away or touching another person's arm to show that you would like a turn to have the floor. The Italian culture is one where there is a lot of physical touch and outsiders might see this as being overly friendly and intimate but in actuality, Italians use such touching because they place great significance on these gestures to send messages in communication. They are smartly trying to restrict the gestures of each other's hands so that they can take the floor. They usually reserve the right hand for demanding that attention while articulating their points and showcasing their emotions with their left hand. Therefore, right-handed people have an upper hand in conversation in this culture. Pun intended!

Handshaking

This gesture is exhibited by people pressing their palms together and shaking their hands up and down an in-pumping action. This is typically a gesture of greeting but the meaning varies depending on how this gesture is performed. For example, the length of time that this is done suggests the meaning. Holding the handshake for too long - more than 3 pumps - can be seen as intimate, while doing it for too short a time normally raises suspicions.

How the palm feels also leaves an impression. For example, a wet palm during a handshake suggests that a person is sweaty because he or she is nervous.

The positioning of the handshake is also important. Shaking the hands evenly with palms facing the other person suggests that a person feels equally toward another. If a person twists the handshake so that their palm is over the other person's, suggests that they feel superior to the other person. Twisting the handshake so that the palm up suggests that a person feels submissive to the other person.

How tightly a person squeezes the other person's palm while shaking hands also makes an impression. Shaking the other person's hand too tightly is seen as a power play to assert dominance while a weak handshake suggests that this person is not only physically weak but also mentally and emotionally weak by comparison.

CHAPTER 7

NONVERBAL OF THE FACE

If hand gestures are some of the fastest-changing nonverbal behaviors, then facial expressions are the most complex. Of course, facial expressions change over time, though not as quickly as hand gestures. What is most challenging about analyzing them is that they can be so nuanced. A small flicker of a look can appear for a moment - what did it mean? Was that an underlying thought bubbling to the surface? A momentary daydream? Facial expressions in their purest forms are simplistic, but it is how we, as human beings, mix possible combinations, which makes them so subtle at times.

> *"Reactive expressions happen when a person is receiving and responding to information"*

How to Analyze People through the Nonverbal Behavior of the Face

Facial expressions can be proactive or reactive. It is through understanding this distinction that you will have a better success rate when analyzing key expression attributes. Dynamic facial expressions occur when they are "sent" out to be received. For example, if someone were to tell you a funny story and they start laughing and smiling as they are saying it - that's a proactive facial expression. It is intended to be received, and usually comes in tandem with a speech that is directed at another person. Do not mistake this for always being conscious of nonverbal communication. It is not. Sometimes a person chooses to smile while talking, but at other times the smile will come through subconsciously. What is essential here is to recognize that the facial expression is being broadcast as part of a message.

Reactive expressions happen when a person is receiving and responding to information. Taking the above example, although the person telling you the funny story is laughing, you start to frown. Why? Because you find the joke to be in poor taste. It again could be an instinctive reaction or one you deliberately broadcast, but what makes it reactive is that the facial expression is in response to something.

Think about these two broad categories of facial expressions as you analyze a person's behavior. Are they responding or sending? If they are sending out a facial expression while talking, then this is more likely to be what they want to be perceived. That does not mean it is accurate. If they are responding, then it is more likely that it is an instinctual response and, therefore, more representative of what is going on in their mind.

Of course, there are ifs, buts, and maybes surrounding these two categories. Sometimes a person can be sending out reactive expressions while talking because they are responding to their own emotions and how their communication is being received. In this way, all we can say about reactive and proactive expressions is that they tend to be presented when switching between receiving and sending messages.

What are Micro Expressions?

When we mentioned the nuance of facial expressions and how subtle they can be, we were referring to micro expressions. These are small movements of the face that reveal the true feelings and thoughts of a person. They are usually involuntary and great examples of emotional impulses from the limbic system pushing past an individual's defenses to being revealed to the outside world.

Facial expressions can be faked (more on that below). However, micro expressions are much more difficult to fake because of their involuntary nature. There are seven established micro-expressions, and each of them is connected to deep, visceral emotion. Be vigilant for each when analyzing someone.

These micro-expressions are:

Surprise: This manifests itself as having raised eyebrows, wrinkled brow, wide-open eyes, and often the jaw-dropping full and showing teeth. The surprise is relatively ambiguous as it can be either a negative response or a positive response.

Hate: Also referred to as contempt, it often presents itself with one side of the mouth raised. There can also be a furrowed brow, but hatred is often accompanied by a blank or apathetic expression.

Sadness: This emotion filters through onto the face with the lips curled down at the sides and a furrowed brow, which arches upward in the middle creating vertical and horizontal lines. The cheeks and muscles around the eyes can be tensed.

Happiness: When a moment of joy flickers across the face, it presents with no wrinkled brow, a smile, raised cheeks, and crow's feet at the sides of the eyes.

Disgust: This has a surprise component, though mixed with disgust. It manifests on the face with raised upper eyelids, curled upper lip with nose wrinkled, and the cheeks raised. It can also present with a furrowed brow, and the corners of the mouth curved downwards.

Anger: This presents itself with eyebrows lowering and furled in the middle. Often vertical lines appear between the eyebrows. Lower lids tense up and raise slightly. Pursed lips. Flaring nostrils. Gritting teeth. A focused stare, and also tilting of the head slightly downward, occasionally upward.

Fear: Perhaps the most instinctive emotion of all. It manifests as raised eyebrows that are curling towards each other in the middle of the brow—which causes the forehead to become wrinkled. As a surprise, the eyes are quite wide, but the lower lids do not pull down as much. The mouth will open with the chin, sometimes pulling in towards the chest.

Sometimes these micro-expressions can be present at the same time or in close proximately, so stay alert to such changes should they occur.

Facial Expressions can be faked!

We have mentioned the importance of deception in nonverbal communication. It is common practice for a deceptive individual to use facial expressions to fake communication or hide what they are thinking. However, as they are so intuitive, only the most seasoned (and sometimes sociopathic) can fake micro-expressions realistically.

That being said, it is essential to keep an eye out for common signs of deception. For example, someone who is smiling widely with their mouth, but their eyelids remain static, is most probably not that happy. Look for combinations of competing for micro expressions. If you see someone smile, but their brow is furrowed as if disgusted, you will see the conflict between what they are trying to show you and what they are thinking.

Isolated Nonverbal Expressions

As well as micro-expressions, there are several expressions and states which can be isolated to parts of the face. These can also help you to detect deception, but can also reinforce your interpretation of another nonverbal cue.

Stay aware of:

Eye Gestures: Just as the hands can make gestures conveying meaning, the eyes can too. Looking away and to the side, while talking, can mean deception as the person is trying to think through what they are saying, but it can also mean the person is trying to remember something. Too much eye contact seems unnatural, and again if someone is never breaking their stare, deception or an attempt at domination is likely. Staring at the ground or focusing on the hands can also be an adapter to alleviate nervousness. A glazed look shows disinterest or daydreaming. Even the dilation of the pupils can tell us something, with overly dilated eyes linked to forms of deception and arousal.

Glasses and Makeup: Remember that how the body interacts with the environment can contain vital clues about intent and desires. If a person wears glasses, for example, they can use these in a way which shows concentration (taking the glasses off and putting one of the arms in the mouth), or dislike (looking over the top of the glasses with the head tilted down). Makeup, which draws attention to the mouth and eyes are often misread as purely to attract a mate, but they are commonly used to portray confidence. In some circumstances, makeup can be an adapter of sorts to help reduce insecurity. The style of makeup used can also tell us how the individual feels about a specific situation in some circumstances (professional vs. personal).

The Lips: We have mentioned how the lips can convey the information above. They can smile when happy or relaxed, the corners can point down when sad or disgusted, and they can tense up or become pursed when stressed or worried.

Nose Flare Displays: Our nostrils flare to take in more air, and this often occurs when our pulse rate quickens. It can be due to anger or arousal.

Furrowed Forehead Display: The eyebrows convey much about how a person is feeling. What is fascinating about them is that with just a small alteration, they can appear to express an opposing emotion. When frowning, the eyebrows draw together, and this brings the forehead into play. When this happens in tandem, we can see annoyance, anger, or deep concentration.

Blushing and Blanching: Blushing has long been associated with feeling embarrassment or feeling attracted to someone. One theory behind the use of blush makeup is that it mimics this signal and therefore attracts people towards it. However, blushing can mean anxiety or a quickening pulse as the capillaries in the face open up. It can also be the case that a person has social worries about blushing, and this exacerbates the issue. It can also be a defensive reaction when deceiving someone. However, some individuals simply have a strong flush response, and that should not be read into much.

Smiles and Laughter: The World's Most Irresistible Gestures

Laughter and smiling are both powerful communicators. As you no doubt, realize by now, they are, like most nonverbal cues, capable of being presented consciously and subconsciously. What is so fascinating about the smile is that it is also the most common means of deception. The main reason it is used for is fraud because people are naturally treated more positively when they smile, in some cases, even receiving more lenient sentences in the courts. It is called the smile leniency effect, and it is why lying through smiling is so commonly attempted.

It is not always easy to spot, but fake smiles can be identified by:

A Lack of Closed Eyes: Smiling brings about changes in the upper face. This includes the eyelids narrowing. If the eyes are wide or cold looking, then the smile is only skin deep.

No Crow's Feet: The orbicularis oculi muscle creates wrinkles around the eyes when we smile. However, when someone is faking a smile, this muscle often does not engage.

Showing Lower Teeth: When someone fakes a smile, they sometimes show their lower teeth. When we smile naturally, the cheekbone major muscle group pulls the smile upward, which means the bottom teeth should fully or partially obscure the lips. If you can see a lot of the lower teeth, this may suggest deception.

Smiles come in many shapes and sizes, but psychologists have identified five main types. By being able to differentiate between them, it is possible to become a far more skillful reader of facial expressions.

The five smile types are:

1. The Seductive Smile: This smile is used to either gain favor or signal attraction. It involves a subtle smile but with extended direct eye contact and then a slow glancing away. It also includes submissive head tilting to the side or downward.

2. Sarcastic Smile: Here, the mouth is upturned as though happy. Sometimes the mouth is a crooked smirk, and there is always a look of mocking disbelief or disdain in the eyes.

3. Fake Smile: We've covered this one extensively.

4. Uncomfortable Smile: This smile is usually born out of nervousness. It is often a way to satisfy someone who has said something you do not agree with, but you do not want to get into a confrontation about it. The smile is often closed-lipped, and the eyebrows raise slightly and curl up in the center.

5. Duchenne Smile: Coined by psychologist Paul Ekman, this smile is the real deal - it expresses real happiness. It is the polar opposite of a fake laugh complete with narrowing eyelids, crow's feet, with the cheeks raised.

CHAPTER 8

HOW TO SPOT EMOTION WITH BODY LANGUAGE

Reading and analyzing people is a skill. Like most skills, some people master them easily while others have to learn. Think about it like coding. Some children master coding skills at an early age, and by the time they hit their teenage years, they are very good at coding and can hack some of the most secure systems. On the other hand, some people learn to code later on in life. They get through life oblivious of their potential in computer science, but when they start learning, they become masters. This is what happens with reading people.

"Reactive expressions happen when a person is receiving and responding to information"

It does not matter when you learn to read people. What matters is how good you are at it and what you do to improve your skills. To be honest, this is an important skill that you will be well suited to learn. It can save you in many situations. You might not be able to read someone's mind, but you can read what you see in their actions and what you hear in their words. That counts for something because you have tangible evidence upon which you base your actions.

In as much as you will learn how to read people, you must also be aware of your weaknesses. Even some of the best analysts out there will, from time to time, struggle to set aside their experiences, unconscious bias, or normal influence and knowledge of human nature.

Before you claim awareness of what someone is thinking, you have to step back and question the basis of your knowledge. Do you have information or evidence to back your analysis? Are you sure you are not projecting your personal experience on the subject to conclude? Of all the information you have about the subject, do you believe you have thoroughly analyzed them all before making a decision? More importantly, is the information in your possession credible and thorough enough to rule out any other possibility behind the subject's behavior? If you can do that, you will have an honest and accurate analysis of the subject.

In many cases, when you believe you have a hunch about someone, it is no more than your personal bias clouding your judgment. From there, you can make an incorrect decision about them, yet deep down, you believe you are correct. Critical thinking must be an important part of such assessments. The ability to read people is a skill, an important one that we should all learn.

It is easier to read some people than others. In a powerful position, it is wise to make the participants feel comfortable. Relax the situation so that they feel comfortable enough to express themselves freely. This way, you have a better chance of analyzing their feelings and thoughts clearer.

How many times have you come across poker face in conversations? People throw it around randomly even when it's not necessary, but it alludes to someone who can conceal their emotions and feelings by keeping a straight face. Such a person can be sad but interact jovially with everyone, masking their deep pain. Many reports suggest that spoken words only account for 7% of communication. Further, they suggest that body language and tonal variation account for 55% and 38% respectively (Wiesenthal, Silbersweig, and Stern, 2016).

While the population samples for these studies might vary from each situation, the concept is true. Therapists and clinical psychologists read so much into their patients' lives by observing their facial expressions and body language while in session. Many patients are defensive and only come to therapy because they are made to. To get out of therapy, they spin tales of how they are doing well already and feeling better and can reintegrate into society. However, the therapist is trained to notice the disconnect between their actions and words.

The therapist will try to find an action pattern at different parts of the conversation, most of them unrelated, and use this to assess whether the patient is honest about their words or not. It is not just about telling whether the patient is healed or not; it is also about helping them heal. A lot of people also come to therapy as a last resort. Everything else has failed them, and they need to find solace in someone or something. By understanding body language, therapists can genuinely show empathy and encourage the patient to stay strong.

This is another technique of creating a healthy environment where the patient can knock down their boundaries and allow the therapist to understand their pain and distress and eventually help them overcome their tribulations.

Let's take another example—parenting. Many parents have a deep (if not intimate) understanding of their children. Despite the brave face that your child might show, you know something is not right. You can feel the depression. You know a certain behavior pattern in your child, and when that pattern changes abruptly, you are wise to know something is amiss.

Many children struggle in life, especially as they approach their teen years. They struggle because they feel no one understands them. This is how they end up finding help in the wrong places because someone was keener on their behavior than the people closest to them. Such people eventually exploit their innocence.

To be fair to parents, understanding and reading teenagers is not easy. They are at a point in their lives where hormonal changes and interaction with the rest of the world conflict with everything that they might have learned about life growing up. It is so confusing for them. Most of them embrace their true identity at this point, and it might be different from what you might have expected of them growing up. As the development advances, their ability to conceal their real feelings also grows, especially if they feel they are going in a different direction than what you expect of them.

CHAPTER 9

HOW TO SPOT A LIE WITH BODY LANGUAGE

The Psychology of Lying

Lies. They have so much more power than we give them credit for. Lies have been responsible for causing trouble, damaging relationships, destroying trust and reputation. Lying involves two parties - the one who is deceiving, and the one who is being deceived. The deceiver, in this case, purposefully communicates the wrong information and gives false impressions deliberately. Throughout our lives, everyone is going to be playing the role of deceiver at some point, and other times, we could be playing the role of the one who is being deceived.

"Our bodies tend to give us away"

Why are we so quick to believe someone's lies at times? Are we just plain gullible? Or do we feel so overwhelmed cognitively that it is simply easier to believe what someone is telling us, rather than search for the truth? University of Virginia's psychologist, Bella DePaulo (Ph.D.) conducted a study and found that lying was in fact, a condition of life. DePaulo's study revealed that most people lied at least once or twice a day. It is as common as brushing your teeth or drinking water. Both men and women did it, and there were some relationships, such as that between a parent and a teenager, in which deception was higher than ever.

We know lying is wrong, yet why do we do it? We use the terms "little white lie" to sometimes even justify our actions and ease our conscience. The simple truth of the matter is, people, lie because they cannot help themselves. It has become almost second nature to us to try and hide the truth when we feel there is a need for it. We use it to bail us out of awkward situations, we use it to strengthen relationships which we know are going to benefit us at some point, we lie to be kind and to spare someone's feelings, we lie to enhance our social standing, and we lie to keep us out of trouble. Lying has become something of a survival mechanism, and that is why humans will always be prone to telling a lie.

Signs Someone Is Lying

Our bodies tend to give us away. There are telltale signs which indicate when someone might be less than honest. Nobody likes being caught in a lie or being told they are a liar. When the lie comes from someone you know, love, or trust, that painful trust can be even more disappointing.

When you get caught lying in a professional setting, that will completely jeopardize your reputation and kill any chance of having a career.

Some scenarios where a person could lie - or be required to lie - include the following:

• *When It's Habitual* - A classic scenario of when someone may habitually lie is when they say "I'm fine" even when they are not. Sometimes, this is done out of courtesy because they don't want to burden someone else with their problems. Other times, it could be because they're so used to saying they're fine that it's on autopilot now and they don't even think about it anymore. They may even lie if they don't want to encourage more questions because they don't feel like talking about it or involving someone else in their problems. Everyone has done this at least several times in their life, where they lie about being fine when they are not.

• *As A Form of Deflection* - Politicians are especially apt at this one, as they rely on extensive use of body language and verbal lies to deflect questions which they don't want to answer. In this scenario, they attempt to deflect you from paying attention to what matters through this form of distraction.

• *When It Is Expected* - In a legal setting is where you would see this happening most often, hence the term plausible deniability. This form of lying is expected, perhaps even customary as part of the job. Certain scenarios such as adhering to nondisclosure agreements and cross-company relationships are an expected part of some jobs. Then some jobs require you to think fast on your feet and respond while simultaneously protecting information. In these scenarios, lying is expected of you. Some people also may feel the need to lie because they don't like revealing their weaknesses to others, and they may try to cover that negative trait by lying and turning it into something positive instead.

Are They Telling Me the Truth?

How do you spot when someone is potentially telling you a lie? Especially when lying can take on so many forms during the day. The answer? By analyzing them and paying exceptional attention to spot when someone is being dishonest with you. When it comes to analyzing people to potentially spot dishonesty, here's what you need to keep in mind:

Observe When They Attempt to Deny: One of the most important things you need to listen to is the direct denial of an accusation. They will attempt to justify or defend themselves instead of directly addressing the question posed to them. They might respite to giving answers such as not likely, not exactly, not for the most part are common examples of what someone might say when they're attempting to deny an accusation. The next time you observe someone not giving you a definitive answer, they might very well be lying for some reason.

Avoid Speculating: Analyzing and speculating are two different things.

When someone crosses their arms, we shouldn't just speculate that they are being closed off or annoyed without analyzing all the facts which are presented in front of us. Crossing the arms in front of the chest is a classic example of a body language gesture which often gets misunderstood because it could hold so many meanings to it. What you should do instead is to analyze the other elements which led to this move. Did this person cross their arms in response to a question? The first sign of deceptive behavior that happens in the first five seconds of the question asked will enable you to determine if that question was the one that produced the folded arms. This first clue of deception could even happen while the first question is being asked, which goes to know that this person's brain is moving much faster than the words coming out of the interviewer - it is a sign that they are subconsciously trying to frame their response. Keep an eye out for clusters of behavior, too, and whether this is a direct response to a question.

Avoid Being Biased: Remember the story of the boy who cried wolf? The little boy was dishonest several times until one day, he was finally telling the truth but nobody believed in him anymore. This story goes to show that even dishonest people are capable of telling truths now and then. To analyze if someone is being dishonest in a situation requires you to focus on the truthful responses they give while filtering out all the other information. Certain individuals are capable of telling truths while simultaneously lying at certain points in their story, and by keeping an eye on the essential information, you avoid being distracted by the untruths in their tale.

Observing When They're Being Evasive: Those who tell tall tales often include a lot of unnecessary fluff and long explanations in their stories, all the while never really addressing the issue at hand. Beating around the bush is how you would best sum it up. Redirecting and deflecting their responses is something they have become adept at doing, and they will try to distract you by even sometimes turning your question into another question. Have I ever done this before? Don't you know me well enough to know that I wouldn't? Don't I have a good reputation? These are just some of the many examples and ways in which someone might act evasively. If you observe that someone is doing this for a good 15 minutes or more and blatantly avoids directly answering your questions, it could be a good indicator that they are trying not to get caught in a lie.

Be On the Lookout for Signs of Aggression: If someone is quick to anger and becomes defensive when asked a question, that raises a red flag that there may be something going on, more than what they are willing to let on. When an individual begins to get defensive, angry, perhaps even aggressive, they may attempt to turn things around and make it seem like you are the one who is in the wrong. They could accuse you of being biased, discriminatory, and more, making it appear as though it was your fault. The blame game is a common technique used by those who are being dishonest.

Observe Their Body Language: And of course, there is the ever-faithful, natural lie detector that never fails - body language. A person's words could tell the most convincing, believable story you've ever heard, but their body will give them away before their minds can catch up. A subtle facial gesture is all it takes to give the game away, and if you're keenly observing them, these clues will be hard to miss. A person could touch their face or nose or even cover their mouth or face because this is another subconscious way of hiding a lie. The stress of deception can also cause the skin to turn cold and start itching or even flush - notice when they suddenly scratch their ears or nose. Look out for anchor point movements such as the changes in the arms or even the feet. Has the person suddenly started tapping their feet nervously? Or sweating profusely?

All of these situations are important to watch and you must also watch the cluster of behaviors and activity as opposed to zoning in on only one behavior. Spotting whether someone is telling a lie or the truth can be hard at first. It certainly requires training to efficiently tell if someone is lying so don't be disheartened because you're not able to do it right away. It is almost impossible.

Studying the Body Language of Liars

Perceiving a falsehood when you hear one can be a generally excellent ability to have throughout everyday life. Perhaps you are tired of finding past the point of no return that somebody has deceived you. Or on the other hand, maybe you are famously guileless and simple to trick. And when you are tired of being deceived, you can build your capacity to perceive a lie with an iota of exertion on your part.

Search for pressed together lips. At the point when an individual lies, their mouth generally winds up dry in the meantime because of the uneasiness and anxiety from lying. Because of this, the liar may press together their lips or make a sucking motion. If you see white on their lips, it's a marker that they are pressing together their lips and might lie.

Notice and when they shield their eyes or mouth. Our cerebrums subliminally give away little intimations through our conduct when we lie. For instance, it is regular for individuals to cover their mouths when they lie or to conceal their eyes from the individual they are lying to.

•If an individual puts their hands to cover their mouth, this can be a marker of a falsehood.

•The most basic way that somebody shields their eyes is by shutting them. This does exclude ordinary squinting – however delayed eye shutting checks.

Watch for anxious squirming. Liars frequently have a spike in tension dimensions since they are apprehensive about concealing the reality and afraid of being caught. The body wants to disperse this tension and it frequently shows in apprehensive squirming of some sort which is a signal to get the hidden emotions on the person's face.

- This can incorporate preparing signals like hauling your hair behind your ear, altering your tie, or rectifying your skirt. These changing positions give an analysis of people's intentions and you should always take note of these changes as they reveal things subconsciously.

- It can likewise incorporate hand to face movements like pulling on your ear or modifying the position of your glasses.

- Additionally, this may show as face language and it reveals more emotions on the outer part of the body. This includes repositioning your telephone or moving a glass of water when conversing with someone.

Watch the movement of their eyes. At the point when individuals are lying, the cerebrum frequently gives little markers through the eyes because the individual is awkward or on edge about saying the truth. Watch for fast squinting or eyes dashing forward and backward as indications of lying.

- Eyes shooting forward and backward show that an individual feels caught and they are searching for an exit plan – this could be both physically (they need to escape the room and make tracks in an opposite direction from the circumstance making them lie) and inwardly (they need to escape coming clean).

- When someone blinks at regular intervals, you should understand what that is passing across. And when somebody blinks more often in a conversation, it could be a marker that they are lying – particularly and when they squint 5 or multiple times quickly in succession.

The art of recognizing sudden changes in Tone and voice

Consider how they speak normally. When you notice an individual more often than not talks gradually and talking in all respects rapidly and confusing their words, it's most likely a sign that they are lying. Watch for changes in verbal conduct as an indication of lying. So, you should always take note of people's words and how they pitch the same, this allows you to know their point of view and what they mean.

•If you are attempting to decide whether an individual is lying and you don't have any acquaintance with them as of then, just pose them a few questions to inquire what you know the response to (like their name or calling. This is to measure how they talk regularly and at that point get some information about the thing you figure they may lie about.

•An individual's typical conduct in low-stress conditions is called their "benchmark." and this shows how the person could control himself. When you notice an inconsistent move in their communication baseline, then you should sense a foul play.

Watch out for people who love distancing themselves. Individuals who lie regularly always find pleasure in attempting to remove themselves from the falsehood. This implies they regularly avoid utilizing individual pronouns about themselves like "I," "me," or "mine." Sometimes they employ the use of these words in the typical discourse, yet watch out for diminished utilization contrasted with how they ordinarily speak.

•Liars may likewise utilize "him" and "her" rather than individuals' names more often in a communication channel and you should take note of this tip when trying to analyze if someone is saying the truth or not.

Look for long-winded responses. Sometimes people who lie give indirect, long-winded responses to straight-forward questions that could have received a simple answer. Rambling is a sign of nervousness that often occurs when someone is lying.

Of course, you should consider the person's normal manner of speaking. Some people just ramble when they speak normally. So, keep this in mind.

Watch their manner when speaking. The liar will seem nervous, speak quite quickly, and want to change the subject or leave as soon as they can. They may get defensive if you repeatedly ask them probing questions such as "Are you sure?" and "Is that the complete truth?" because they want to deflect attention away from the lie.

What to do to make lies obvious

As far as I can tell, individuals who pose this extremely summed up an inquiry, dependably have quite certain worries as a primary concern.

Noting all these in a manner helpful to you will necessitate that you uncover more in the method for particulars.

For instance, the motivation behind why a given explicit individual tells a ton of falsehoods can be anything from obsessive causes (dysfunctional behavior) and commitment to winning through double-dealing.

Yet, and when you are attempting to make sense of why we go over varieties of individuals who lie in a general manner, the reasons will be extraordinary. For instance, some basic human collaborations are socially planned around individuals misleading one another, more often than not in generally innocuous ways.

In early social communications, loads of more youthful individuals will in general untruth since they learn (kind of coincidentally) as little youngsters, that getting anything they need that grown-ups don't need them to have (which would incorporate sex), is most effectively increased through falsehoods. They frequently believe that lying is a flat out need.

Pose testing inquiries. The more inquiries you pose to them, particularly questions requiring profundity and detail, the more awkward they will move toward becoming because they should make up to an ever-increasing extent. They may repudiate themselves or lead themselves into a trap.

• It is extremely difficult to totally create a nitty-gritty story on the spot so search for chinks in their defensive layer. And when you truly give them an exhaustive round of questioning they may even in the long run disintegrate and concede they are lying (however don't depend too vigorously on this occurrence).

• Ask them a few times to clarify the succession of occasions. This is difficult to keep straight for somebody who is lying and it is likely they will commit an error.

• Ask them little insights regarding the thing they're lying about – like what shading their shirt was or how they felt when they saw somebody.

• Consider past direct and offenses. In case the individual you consider lying has lied already, they will undoubtedly lie now. Think about how the individual would ordinarily act in this condition and balance it with their theorized lie.

• For precedent, and when you are an educator and you think your understudy is lying concerning why they haven't gotten their work done once more, contrast their reason with past reasons to check whether they constantly will, in general, be detailed, outlandish, or identified with a specific reason.

• Ask the liar for any kind of help. In case you're experiencing difficulty making sense of something, a legitimate individual will enable you to conceptualize to concoct an answer. A liar won't have any desire to give you a larger number of subtleties or data than they are required to.

•Try posing inquiries like, "Would you be able to consider any other person who may have approached this PC?" If the individual attempts to enable you to make sense of another probability, they are most likely coming clean. Yet, and when they state they have no clue or respond adversely/forcefully, they are likely lying.

When the Face Gives the Game Away

Our faces are one of the most revealing, honest parts of our bodies. Without saying a word, your face can convey every emotion with such depth that people will be able to tell what you're feeling if it is expressed strongly. Crying, laughing, frowning, stress, anxious, depressed, nervous, all of these emotions flash across our faces when we feel them within us. Sometimes, even though we may want to cover up our feelings, our bodies don't necessarily cooperate, and our expressions become apparent on our faces for anyone observant to notice.

It is the signals in our body that will reveal the truth at the end of the day. Most of the time, we are completely unaware that our face is giving the game away. We may think we're doing a good job of covering up our emotions and putting on a mask, but without even realizing it, a slight slip of the mask is all it takes for the truth to snake its way out.

The reason why our faces are incapable of hiding the truth is because of the conflicting emotions that are happening within us. Whenever we're occupied with trying to tell a lie, certain thoughts may be going through our minds simultaneously. It is these thoughts that are shown for a split second across our faces. This is what gives us away. This split-second emotion is what reveals the way that we truly feel.

Why is it so difficult to tell a lie? Because our subconscious mind knows what's truly going on and it is acting independently from the verbal lie that we are telling everyone else. This is why our body language becomes out of sync with the words we are saying because our mind is not working in sync. Those who rarely tell a lie are the ones who are most easily caught. Since they haven't had much practice, their bodies don't know how to respond fast enough to the contradictory lie that they are telling, which makes their body language signals even more obvious than ever. They may believe that they have been convincing, but their bodies are telling a completely different story through a nervous gesture or a facial twitch which accompanies the lie.

Certain people have mastered the art of lying so well that they are much harder to spot. People like lawyers, politicians, actors, TV personalities, and even professional liars, for example, have perfected their technique and refined their body language gestures to a point where their lies become a lot harder to spot. People believe these individuals a lot more easily because the lies are harder to see. How did they accomplish this seemingly miraculous feat of being able to trick the body into not revealing a lie? They spend time practicing. They practice what they think feels like the right gestures when they tell a lie, and this long-term practice has been done over a long time. They have also practice minimizing their gestures, forcing themselves to keep their bodies calm and neutral when they're lying. It isn't easy, but it is certainly doable through lots and lots of practice.

Spotting a Lie - The Most Common Gestures Used

Certain gestures are used more than others during a lie. When you learn how to recognize them, that's when you start recognizing all the other cues to look out for which the lying individual may be displaying. Here are some of the most commonly used gestures during a lie, so the next time you suspect someone may be untruthful to you, see if you can spot the following telltale signs:

Covering the Mouth – Subconsciously, our brain is trying to tell us to stop the lies that are coming out of our mouths. Our bodies know what we're saying isn't true, and the mind is trying to prevent or resist the act of lying, which is why some people inadvertently put their hands across their mouths. An act of trying to "cover up a lie". This gesture can sometimes manifest in the form of someone trying to fit their fist into their mouth, too. Some people even try to cover up this gesture by pretending to cough. Actors often assume this gesture when they are playing the parts of criminals in movies or TV shows. When the "criminal" gets caught, the actors subtly incorporate this gesture into their acting like their way of cueing the audience in that they are being deceitful and dishonest. If someone uses this gesture when they are speaking, it could be indicative of a lie. If someone exhibits this gesture when you are speaking, it could be that they feel you are hiding something. We even see this gesture being exhibited in children at times, through the innocuous "shhh" where one finger is placed over the lips to indicate a secret. The next time you notice this gesture in someone, keep an eye out because something may be amiss in their story.

Nose Touch - Some people may rub their noses quickly. Some may just rub their nose in one, quick motion which may be almost imperceptible. Whether this indicates someone is fibbing or not would depend on the context. Sometimes, they could be feeling unwell, or their nose could be itchy when certain elements are present. Research conducted by the Smell and Taste Treatment and Research Foundation revealed that when a person lies, a particular chemical which is known as catecholamines gets released. This chemical is then responsible for the swelling of the nose, especially during intentional lying. This is also the chemical that causes someone's blood pressure to increase. When our noses swell thanks to the blood pressure, we're left with a "tingling" sensation which results in an itch in the nose, which explains why some people briskly rub their noses when they're lying. Almost as though they were trying to scratch an itch. Analyzing Bill Clinton's testimony on his affair with Monica Lewinsky, it is noticeable that Clinton rarely ever touched his nose when he was lying. However, when he did lie, there would be a slight frown that lasted only for a split second, followed by a quick nose touch. How do you distinguish between when someone is lying and when they just have an itchy nose? Well, when someone is generally experiencing a nose itch, they will deliberately scratch or rub their nose, whereas those who use the lying gesture involves light strokes to the nose.

Eye Rub - The rubbing of the eyes is our subconscious brain's way of trying to block out what we perceive to be deceitful or distasteful. Men tend to do this more so than women, who will usually exhibit this move in the form of gentle touch motions just below the eye area. Some people exhibit the eye rub maneuver when they want to avoid looking at a person directly in the eye because they know they are lying to them.

Ear Grab - Have you ever spotted someone tugging at their earlobe when they answer a question? This gesture is sometimes associated with the act of lying, but at other times, it could be indicative of other things. This gesture is also exhibited by a person who is experiencing anxiety. Again, this move would depend on the context in which it is exhibited. In Italy, for example, the ear grab means something different entirely and is used to signal when someone is effeminate or gay.

Neck Scratch - This often accompanies the ear-grabbing signal. A person who is lying could exhibit this move by scratching the side of their neck just below the earlobe (if they don't do the earlobe move). This gesture is not only used when someone is telling a lie but also gets displayed when they are feeling doubtful or unsure about something. It can be a very telling sign if it is accompanied by verbal cues that contradict this gesture. For instance, if a person says yes, I can understand where you're coming from but accompanies it with a neck scratch, this could be an indicator that they do not understand at all, and they are just agreeing with you for the sake of doing so.

CHAPTER 10

BEHAVIOR ANALYSIS

When Talking About Behavior Analysis, we focus on using learning principles to bring behavioral change. This is a branch of psychology that aims to understand the unforeseen cognitions and focuses on the behavior of a person and not on the mental causes of said behavior.

Behavior analysis has extremely fruitful practical applications when it comes to mental clarity and health, especially in helping children and adults learn a new sense of behaviors or reduce certain problematic behaviors.

> "We get angry when nobody, especially someone close to us doesn't notice that we are angry"

Analyzing Social Behaviors

The intentions behind certain actions of ours are commonly hidden. When a person is feeling angry or feeling depressed for example, their behavior portraying this feeling is usually very different such as they would keep quiet or go for a smoke to calm down.

Another example is also the kind of words used to convey dissatisfaction such as 'sure, go ahead' or 'fine' when we are not fine with the solution or the decision made. Empathy is much-needed when it comes to analyzing social behaviors such as this because, at the end of the day, you want to understand and listen and not just hear to answer.

In analyzing behaviors, demonstrating trust, and building rapport are extremely crucial because when you display empathy, you naturally break down any subversions and focus on the heart of the matter.

A rule to remember is that when you do experience emotions and feelings, you must know that people around you will not know about it unless they sense a change in your body language. When nobody understands or gets it, there is no need to get angry—but of course, it is easier said than done. We get angry when nobody, especially someone close to us doesn't notice that we are angry.

Behavior Is Largely Dictated By Selfish Altruism.

Nobody is completely selfish and if we were to make such a claim, that would mean we are ignoring the acts of sacrifice, kindness, and love that go around the world. However, most behavior does come out from the elements of selfish altruism.

It is a win/win situation when it comes to selfish altruism. It is a basic two-way road of you help me, I will help you. Here are a few scenarios where selfish altruism applies:

1. Transactions: If you were to purchase a car, both the seller and

the buyer mutually benefit. The buyer gets the vehicle; the seller gets their sales. This is a primary form of selfish altruism between two people who do not have any kind of emotional bond.

2. Familial: Our mind is designed to protect the people with whom we share our genes. We have a higher tendency to protect these people and this sense of protectiveness depends on close friends to loved ones to siblings and family.

3. Status: People sometimes, not all the time, help someone as a sign of power. Sometimes, people offer assistance and help to boost their reputation and self-esteem.

4. Implied Reciprocity: Plenty of relationships are based on the fact that if I assist you one day, you would remember it and help me out as well one day when I need it.

Some certain behaviors are not part of the categories described above. For example, nameless heroes dying for a cause that does not directly benefit their country or bloodline. Another example is volunteers who devote their time selflessly towards missions and aids. But of course, these are just the smaller portion of the entire world community.

The motives of people and what appeals to them is what you need to understand. When you do, you find ways to help people within these four categories. It's very rare not to expect people to give aid that does not benefit them in any form or way.

People Have Poor Memories.

Not everyone has a bad memory, but our minds have both long-term memory storage and short-term memory storage. For example, ever been introduced to someone at a party and then you just forgot their name the day after? People have trouble remembering things, especially something not relevant to be stored in their long-term memory. People are more likely to remember similarities that they share with you rather than differences.

When analyzing people, remember that people generally forget things so do not assume that they are disinterested with the information you have given or have malice against you.

People Are Emotional.

People have stronger feelings about certain things more than they let on but they can't show their specific emotions too much, especially negative emotions such as anger, outbursts, and depression simply because it is generally frowned upon by society. The rule is not to assume everything is fine just because someone isn't having an outburst. Sometimes the strongest ones are the ones that suffer most. All of us have some form of a problem, and these issues are normally contained. You necessarily do not need to call people out on their private deception, but what you need to do is be a little sensitive to those unseen currents and empathize with people because this gives you an advantage when you are trying to help.

People Are Lonely.

When you look at all these Instagram influencers having the time of their life or even celebrities going to numerous parties and ceremonies, the last thing you'd think is that they are lonely. The reality is, many people who seem like they have it all are quite lonely. People are sensitive to threats of being left out or ostracized or even having the fear of missing out. Loneliness and the desire to be among people exist in all of us, even if we are introverts. Analyzing this behavior is knowing that loneliness is very common among people and in this sense, you're not alone in feeling this way.

People Are Self-Absorbed.

Like it or not, people tend to be more concerned about themselves than about other people. Just look at social media and you can see how self-absorbed people are especially with an account full of selfies. People are more concerned more about themselves to give you any attention and for people to be lonelier, more emotional, and feel different than they let on depends also on how you see the world. This perspective makes you independent and also proactive at the same time when you think about it. You become independent so you do not have to rely on anyone and you are more proactive so you have things to do and places to go on your own without depending on enjoying good times with other people. You place your happiness in your hand rather than in the hands of other people.

When analyzing people, just remember that in some ways or another, they all think and act like you in varying degrees.

CHAPTER 11

COMMON PATTERNS OF INTERPRETING BEHAVIOR

Human behavior is a complex thing. Because of its complexity, reading and analyzing people is not as easy as it sounds—but neither is it hard simply because as human beings, we exhibit more or less the same kinds of mannerisms and behavior when we experience a certain emotion or action.

> *"Think of actions as a form of transition or even an initiation from one situation to another"*

So What Exactly Is Behavior?

Essentially, scientists categorize human behavior into three components:

- Actions
- Cognition
- Emotions

Actions Are Behavior.

An action is regarded as everything that constitutes movement and observation whether using your eyes or using physiological sensors. Think of actions as a form of transition or even an initiation from one situation to another. When it comes to behavioral actions, these can take place at different scales and they range from sweat gland activity, sleep, or food consumption.

Cognitions Are Behavior.

Cognitions are described as mental images that are imprinted in our minds and these images are both nonverbal and verbal. Verbal cognitions are such as thinking 'Wow, I wonder what it's like to wear a $2000-dollar designer dress' or 'I have to get the groceries done later' all constitute verbal cognition. However, imagining things, in contrast, is considered nonverbal cognition, such as how your body will look after losing weight or how your house will be after a repaint. Cognition is a combination of knowledge and skills and knowing how to skillfully use them without hurting yourself.

Emotions Are Behavior.

Emotion is any brief conscious experience that is categorized by intense mental activity and this feeling is not categorized as coming from either knowledge or reasoning. This emotion commonly occurs or exists on a scale starting with positive vibes such as pleasurable to negative vibes such as being unpleasant. Other elements of physiology indicate emotional processing—such as an increase in respiration rate, retina dilation, and even increase in heart rat—all a result of increased or heightened arousal. These elements are usually invisible to the naked eye. Emotions, similar to cognitions also cannot be noticeable to the naked eye. These can only be noticed through tracking facial electromyography activity (FEMG) indirectly which monitors the arousal using ECG, analyzes facial expressions, respiration sensors, galvanic skin response as well as other self-reported measures.

Everything Is Connected

Cognitions, emotions, and actions run together and simultaneously with one another. This excellent synergy enables us to understand the events, activities, and happenings that are happening around us, to get in touch with our internal beliefs and desires, and to correctly or appropriately respond to people that are in this scenario.

It is not that easy to understand and determine what exactly is the effect and cause. For example, when you turn your head, which is an action, and seeing a face familiar to you, this will cause a burst of joy, which is the emotion and is usually accompanied by the realization which is the cognition. In other words, it is through this equation:

ACTION = EMOTION (joy) + cognition (realization)

In some other scenarios, this chain of effect and cause can also be reversed – you may be sad (experiencing an emotion) and you proceed to contemplate on relationship concerns (you go through cognition) and then you proceed to go for a run to clear your mind (you take an action). In this case, the equation would be:

EMOTION (SADNESS) + cognition (I need to go for a run) = action

CONSCIOUS + UNCONSCIOUS behavior

Consciousness is an awareness of our internal thoughts and feelings and it also has to do with proper perception for and the processing of information gathered from our surroundings. A big portion of our behaviors is through the guided unconscious processes that surround us. Like an iceberg, there is a huge amount of hidden information and only a small fraction of it is obvious to our naked eye.

Overt + Covert behavior

Overt behavior focuses on the aspects of behavior that can be observed by the naked eye. These behaviors are such as body movements, or as some would call it–interactions. Physiological processes such as facial expressions, blushing, smiling and pupil dilation may be subtle but it all can still be seen. Covert expressions are thoughts or cognition, feelings which are emotions and responses that are not easily or visibly seen. These subtle changes in our body's responses are usually not seen by the observer's eye.

If we want to observe covert responses, then physiological or biometric sensors are usually used to help in observing them.

Rational + irrational behaviors

Any action, cognition, or emotion which is guided or influenced by reason is considered rational behavior. Irrational behavior, in contrast, is any action, emotion, or cognition that is not objectively logical. For example, people who have extreme phobias are considered as having irrational fears, which are fears that are cause them to behave a certain way.

Voluntary + involuntary behaviors

When an action is self-determined or driven by decisions and desires, this is often categorized as voluntary actions. Involuntary on the other action would be actions that are done without intent, by force, or done in an attempt to prevent it. People who are in cognitive-behavioral psychotherapy are often exposed to problematic scenarios involuntary as a form of therapy so that they can help get through this fear with the help of the therapist at hand. Now that we have a form of understanding of human behaviors, here is how we can interpret these behaviors. Keep in mind that these are just the surface or basic ways that interpretation can be done as there are more other complex and detailed ways.

#1 Establish a baseline

When you read people, you would notice that they all have unique patterns and quirks of behavior. Some people look at the floor while talking, or they have a habit of crossing their arms, some clear their throat ever so often while some pout, jiggle, or squint even. However, these actions could also mean anger, deception, or nervousness. When reading people, we first need to form a baseline by understanding context and also what normal behavior is for this person.

#2 Look for behavior deviations

When you have established baseline behaviors, your next goal is to pay close attention to the inconsistencies that show up between the baseline mannerisms and the person's words and gestures. Say for example you've noticed that your teammate usually twirls their hair when they are nervous. As your teammate starts their presentation, they start to do this. Is this common behavior in your teammate's mannerisms or is there more than meets the eye? You might want to do a little bit more digging and probe a little bit more than you normally would.

#3 Start noticing a collection of gestures

A solitary word or gesture does not necessarily mean anything but when there are a few behavioral patterns that start forming, you need to pay attention to them. It could be that your teammate starts clearing their throat in combination with twirling their hair. Or they keep shifting. This is where you need to proceed with caution.

#4 Compare and contrast

So we go back to the teammate again and you've noticed that they are acting more odd than usual. You move your observation a little closer to see when and if your teammate repeats this behavior with other people in your group. Observe how they interact with the rest of the people in the room and how their expression changes, if at all. Look at their body language and their posture.

#5 Reflect

This reflection isn't about meditation rather it is to reflect the other person's state of mind. As human beings, we have mirror neurons that act like built-in monitors wired to read another person's body language simply because we have these mannerisms as well. For example, a smile activates the smile muscles in our faces whereas a frown activates the frown muscles. When we see someone that we like, our facial muscles relax, our eyebrows arch, our blood flows to our lips making them full and our head tilts. However, if your partner does not mirror this set of behavior, then it could be that they are sending a clear message which is they are not as happy to see you.

#6 identifying the resonant voice

You might think that the most powerful person is the one that sits at the head of the table or the one that is standing in the front. That is not always the case. The most confident person always has a stronger voice and they are more likely the most powerful one. Just by looking at them, you can deduce they have an expansive posture, they have a big smile, and a strong voice. However, make no mistake that a loud voice is not a strong one. If you are presenting to an audience or pitching an idea to a group of people, you would normally focus on the leader. What happens when the leader has a weak personality? They will depend on others to make a decision and they are easily influenced by them. So when pitching or presenting to a group, identify the strong voice and you'll have a stronger chance of success.

#7 Observe how they walk

People who shuffle along or lack a flowing motion in their movements or always keep their head down while walking lack self-confidence. If you see this exhibited by a member of your team, you might be inclined to make extra effort to recognize their contribution to building this person's confidence. You might also need to ask them more direct questions at meeting so that they are inclined to offer their ideas out in the open as opposed to keeping them quiet.

#8 Using action words

Words are usually the closest way for people to understand what is going on in another person's mind. These words symbolize the thoughts that are running through their mind and in identifying these words, you also identify their meaning. Say for example if your friend says 'I decided to make this work', the action word used here is 'Decided'. This solitary word shows that your friend is 1 – not impulsive, 2 – went through a process of weighing the pros and cons, and 3 – Took time to think things through. These actions words offer insight into how a person processes a scenario and thinks.

#9 look for personality clues

Each one of us human beings has a unique personality and these rudimentary classifications can enable us to assess and relate to another person. It also helps us read someone accurately. In looking for clues, you can ask:

- Did this person exhibit more introverted or extroverted behavior?

- Do they seem driven by significance or relationships?

- How do they handle risks and uncertainty?

- What drives them or feeds their ego?

- What kinds of mannerisms does this person exhibit when they are stressed?

- What are the types of mannerisms shown when they are relaxed?

By observing a person long enough, you can pinpoint their base behaviors and mannerisms and set apart the odd one out.

CHAPTER 12

READING PEOPLE THROUGH THEIR HANDWRITING

Every person's handwriting is known to be as unique as their personality. You can make an in-depth analysis of everything from their behavior to personality to the thought process. Graphology is the science of studying an individual's personality through how they write. Handwriting goes beyond putting a few characters on paper. It is about glimpsing into an individual's mind to decipher what they are thinking and how they are feeling based on their handwriting.

Here are some little-known secrets about speed reading a person through their handwriting.

> *"Every person's handwriting is known to be as unique as their personality"*

Reading Letters of the Alphabet

How a person writes his or her letters offer a huge bank of information about their personality, subconscious thoughts, and behavioral characteristics. There are several ways of writing a single letter and every person has a distinct way of constructing it.

For example, putting a dot on the lower case "I" is an indication of an independent-spirited personality, originality, and creative thinking. These folks are organized, meticulous, and focused on details. If the dot is represented by an entire circle, there are pretty good chances of the person being more childlike and thinking outside the box. How a person constructs their upper case "I" reveals a lot about how they perceive themselves. Does their "I" feature the same size as the other letters or is it bigger/smaller compared to other letters?

A person who constructs a large "I" is often egoistic, self-centered, overconfident, and even slightly cocky. If the "I" is the size of other letters or even smaller than other letters, the person is more self-assured, positive, and happy by disposition.

Similarly, how people write their lower case "t" offers important clues into their personality. If the "t" is crossed with a long line, it can be an indication of determination, energy, passion, zest, and enthusiasm. On the other hand, a brief line across the "t" reveals a lack of empathy, low interest, and determination. The person doesn't have very strong views about anything and is generally apathetic. If a person crosses their "t" really high, they possess an increased sense of self-worth and generally have ambitious objectives.

Similarly, people who cross their "t" low may suffer from low self-esteem, low confidence, and lack of ambition. A person who narrows the loop in lower case "e" is likelier to be uncertain, suspicious, and doubtful of people. There is an amount of skepticism involved that prevents them from being trustworthy of people. These people tend to have a guarded, stoic, withdrawn, and reticent personality. A wider loop demonstrates a more inclusive and accepting personality. They are open to different experiences, ideas, and perspectives.

Next, if an individual writes their "o" to form a wide circle, they are most likely people who very articulate, expressive, and won't hesitate to share secrets with everyone. Their life is like an open book. On the contrary, a closed "o" reveals that the person has a more private personality and is reticent by nature.

Cursive Writing

Cursive writing gives us clues about people that we may otherwise miss through regular writing. It may offer us a more comprehensive and in-depth analysis of an individual's personality.

How does a person construct their lower case cursive "l?" If it has a narrow loop, the person is mostly feeling stressed, nervous, and anxious. Again, a wider loop can be a sign that the individual doesn't believe in going by the rule book. There is a tendency to rewrite the rules. They are laidback, low on ambition, and easy-going.

Again, consider the way a person writes cursive "y" to gain more information about their personality. The length and breadth of the letter "y" can be extremely telling. A thinner and slimmer "y" can be an indication of a person who is more selective about their friend circle. On the other hand, a thicker "y" reveals a tendency to get along with different kinds of people. These are social beings who like surrounding themselves with plenty of friends.

A long "y" is an indication of travel, adventure, thrills, and adventures. On the other hand, a brief cursive "y" reflects a need to seek comfort in the familiar. They are most comfortable in their homes and other known territories. A more rounded "s" is a signal of wanting to keep their near and dear ones happy. They'll always want their loved ones to be positive and cheerful.

They will seldom get into confrontations and strive to maintain a more balanced personality. A more tapering "s" indicates a curious, and hard-working personality.

They are driven by ideas and concepts. Notice how cursive "s" broadens at the lower tip. This can be a strong indication of the person being dissatisfied with their job, interpersonal relationships, and or life in general. They may not pursue their heart's true desires.

Letter Size

This is a primary observation that is used for analyzing a person through their handwriting. Big letters reveal that the person is outgoing, affable, gregarious, and extrovert. They are more social by nature and operate with a mistaken sense of pride. There is a tendency to pretend to be something they aren't. On the contrary, tiny letters can indicate a timid, reticent, introverted, and shy personality. It can indicate deep concentration and diligence. Midsized letters mean that an individual is flexible, adjusting, adaptable, and self-assured.

Gaps between Text

People who leave a little gap in between letters and words demonstrate a fear of leading a solitary life. These people always like to be surrounded by other folks and often fail to respect the privacy and personal space of other people. People who space out their words/letters are original thinkers and fiercely independent. For them, they place a high premium on freedom and independence. There is little tendency for being overwhelmed by other people's ideas, opinions, and values.

Letter Shapes

Look at the shape of an individual's letters while decoding their personality. If the writing is more rounded and in a looped manner, the person tends to be high on inventiveness and imagination! Pointed letters demonstrate that a person is more aggressive and intelligent. The person is analytical, rational, and a profound thinker. Similarly, if the letters of an alphabet are woven together, the individual is methodical, systematic, and orderly. They will rarely work or live in chaos.

Page Margin

If you thought it's only about writing, think again. Even the amount of space people leave near the edge of the margin determines their personality. Someone who leaves a big gap on the right side of the margin is known to be nervous and apprehensive about the future.

People who write all over the page are known to have a mind full of ideas, concepts, and thoughts. They are itching to do several things at once and are constantly buzzing with ideas.

Slant Writing

Some people show a marked tendency for writing with a clear right or left slant while other people write impeccably straight letters. When a person's letters slant towards the right, he or she may be affable, easy-going, good-natured, and generally positive. These people are flexible, open to change, and always keen on building new social connections.

Similarly, people who write slanting letters that lean towards the left are mostly introverts who enjoy their time alone. They aren't very comfortable being in the spotlight and are happy to let others hog the limelight. Straight handwriting indicates rational, level-headed, and balanced thinking. The person is more even-tempered, grounded, and ambivalent.

There is a tiny pointer here to avoid reading people accurately. For left-handed people, the analysis is the opposite. When left-handed people have their letters slanting to the right, they are shy, introverted, and reserved. However, if their letters slant to the left, they may be outgoing, gregarious, and social extroverts.

Writing Pressure

The intensity with which an individual writes is also an indicator of their personality. If the handwriting is too intense and full of pressure (there is indentation), the individual may be fiery, aggressive, obstinate, and volatile. They aren't very open to other people's ideas, beliefs, and opinions. There is a tendency to be rigid about their views.

On the contrary, if a person writes with little pressure or intensity, they are likely to be empathetic, sensitive, and considerate towards other people's needs. These people tend to be kind, enthusiastic, passionate, lively, and intense.

Signature

A person's signature reveals plenty about an individual's personality. If it isn't comprehensible, it is a sign that he or she doesn't share too many details about themselves. They fiercely guard their private space and are reticent by nature. On the contrary, a more conspicuous and legible signature is an indication of a self-assured, flexible, transparent, assured, confident, and satisfying personality. They are generally content with what they've accomplished and displayed a more positive outlook on life.

Some people scrawl their signature quickly, which can be an indication of them being impatient, restless, perpetually in a hurry, and desiring to do multiple things at one time. A carefully written and neatly-organized signature is an indication of the person being diligent, well-organized, and precision-oriented.

Signatures that finish in an upward stroke demonstrate a more confident, fun-loving, ambitious, and goal-oriented personality. These people thrive on challenges and aren't afraid of chasing these dreams. Similarly, signatures that finish with a downward stroke are an indication of a personality that is marked by low self-esteem, lack of self-confidence, low ambition, and a more inhibited personality. These folks are likelier to be bogged down by challenges and may not be too goal-oriented.

Stand Out Writing

If a particular piece of writing stands out from the other text, look at it carefully to understand an individual's personality.

For example, if the text is generally written in a more spread out and huge writing, with only some parts of the text stuck together, the person may most likely to be an uncertain, dishonest, or mistrustful individual, who is trying to conceal some important information.

Concluding

Though studying an individual's handwriting can offer you accurate insights about his or her personality, it isn't completely fool-proof. Several other factors are to be taken into consideration to analyze a person accurately. It has its shortcomings and flaws. At times, people may write in a hurried manner, which can impact their writing. Similarly, the way people construct their resume or application letter may dramatically vary from how they may write a to-do list or love letter.

If you want an accurate reading of someone's personality, consider different personality analysis methods like reading verbal and non-verbal communication techniques. Various techniques may offer you a highly in-depth, insightful, precise, and comprehensive method of understanding a person's inherent personality.

CHAPTER 13

WHAT IS BODY "MIRRORING"?

One of the critical roles of mirroring the body language of the target person is that it alerts them that you are taking a deliberate interest in the person and want to strike a rapport with the person. Mirroring helps create a connection between the participating parties in a conversation. Akin to any other aspect of communication, one needs to learn the right way of mirroring body language to realize the maximum benefits of the concept.

> *"It is important to take into consideration your relationship with the target person when mirroring"*

First, start by building your connection through fronting. In fronting, you want to lend the other person, complete attention. Go ahead and square your body so that you are directly facing the target person and try to make them the focus of your universe. Then establish eye contact, which may first appear invasive. Eye contact is critical in communicating your level of interest in the target person by communicating that you are giving undivided attention. Eye contact is also thought to elicit warm feelings that enhance a close connection. You should go ahead and initiate the triple nod, which does two functions. When one does the triple nod, then the target person is likely to speak three or four times longer, making them feel that they are being listened to or what they are communicating is important. Additionally, if one nods, then it communicates that you are in tandem with what the person is saying, and this creates a receptive environment for sustained communication. One should elicit questions that will invite nodding. For instance, start by asking if the weather is warm. Then, pretend, followed by not pretending. In this instance, you are fronting the target person and initiating the right eye contact, and applying the triple nod will help strike a rhythm with the individual. In this instance, you are likely feeling a strong connection, but to realize its full benefit try using the power of imagination by pretending the target person is the most interesting individual you have ever met. Try to imagine it and act accordingly followed by ceasing the pretense. In all this, significant levels of mirroring are likely to happen naturally on its account, but the following techniques can help enhance the mirroring of body language to attain intended goals.

Relatedly, exploit the pace and volume as many times people think of mirroring body language as mimicking the physical actions. However, mirroring body language includes all aspects of nonverbal communication, such as pace and volume. For instance, mirroring the pace and volume of the target person's speech will help initiate a connection and rhythm between the two. If the target person is, a fast talker and loud then enhance your volume and animation and if they are soft and slow, then relax and match them at their level instead. Compared to physical actions, mimicry, pace, and volume matching are easier. Recall how you felt when one of your friends adjusted their pace and volume of speaking to match yours at those instances you probably felt that they want to hold a conversation with you.

Additionally, identify the target person punctuator. Assuming that you have been carefully paying attention to the target person, you are mirroring all this time; then you will notice their favorite punctuator that he or she uses to emphasize a point. For instance, it could be an eyebrow flash such as quickly raising the eyebrows. The punctuator could also be a form of hand gesture, such as the one certain politicians use. For instance, it could be that each time the target person insists on an issue, he or she makes a certain finger gesture, then you can encourage the individual by nodding when he or she makes the particular sign. After his or her submission, you should mimic that gesture to suggest that you align with the submitted views. In all these interactions, you will not utter a single word but are connecting and communicating with the target person.

Equally important, you should test the connection with the target person in several ways. For instance, make an overt unrelated action to the conversation and observe if it is reflected. An example is where you are giving a keynote speech, and a member of the audience comes up to you, and you discuss the similarities that he and you had with your fathers that had both participated in World War

II. At that instance, while talking, you get an irritating itch on your nose that you quickly scratch but then you realize that he reached up and scratched up his nose all the while continuing with his story. Even though it seemed out of place, you go ahead to evaluate if the test was a fluke and a moment later, you scratch your head, and suddenly the target person does the exact thing. It appears odd, and you almost laughed aloud. It is important to avoid repeated testing as it will break the connection and make the entire exercise appear like a prank against the best of your intention. It is also necessary to only mirror positive body language and avoid mirroring negative nonverbal communication such as turning away, closing your eyes, locking with your arms folded, or looking away. Akin to any other aspect of communication, comprehensive practice is important for one to attain efficacy levels.

As indicated, mirroring helps create a rhythm with the target individual. The main intention of mirroring the nonverbal communication of the target person is to make them notice you and fall to your pace of communication—nonverbal communication. Recall your school days when in a sporting activity or a hall with a visiting school. One of the ways that you initiated a conversation was by looking directly at the eyes of the other student that you did not know, and he or she responded. You then slowed your breathing and blinking of eyes to mimic the target student until you felt as if you are talking to each other using words. All these actions constitute mirroring to create a pattern of communication nonverbally with the target person.

For instance, if you smile at a child, it is likely to smile back at you. A common example of mirroring is when you look at your baby or any baby directly in the eyes or smile at them. In most cases, the babies will replicate the same action that you paused at them. For instance, if you clap your hands, they will also clap their hands at you. Though for the case of babies, they may lack the conscious level to perceive what they are doing, it represents the efficiency of mirroring body language. Babies with difficulties reflecting your actions can suggest that something is amiss, enabling you to investigate their welfare deeper.

Compared to men, women are more likely to mirror each other with ease. It emerges that women are likely to mirror the actions of another woman enabling two strangers, women, to connect instantly. If you are a woman or have female friends, then you must have noticed that women appear to easily connect, and it is largely due to mirroring the body language of each other. For instance, if one of the women adjusts her hair, then the other is also likely to the same, and all these increase the likelihood of striking a rapport and creating a rhythm.

It is important to take into consideration your relationship with the target person when mirroring. When mirroring the target person's actions remember that the power relationship between the two of you. For instance, mirroring your supervisor may not be a good idea. At the same time, mirroring a colleague of the opposite sex may be misinterpreted to mean that you are attempting to flirt with them even if they are responding to the mimicry. Similarly, mirroring in some contexts may appear unprofessionally and a violation of work ethics. For instance, a teacher mirroring a student or a doctor mirroring a patient may appear as a mockery even if that is not the intention. Overall, the power relationship with the target person should mediate and moderate the level of body language mirroring.

As such, mirroring body language is an efficient way of building trust and understanding fast. From all these what we learn is that mirroring body language helps initiate trust between two people, especially where the two have a passive history of interaction. As indicated earlier on, you might use mirroring body language during a random interaction such as a sporting event, a party, and any social function where you want to initiate communication and rhythm of communication to build a long-term relationship. In a way, mirroring body language acts as a technique of testing waters before one can verbalize their intentions. Chances are that if the mirroring of body language backfires then the person is likely to the walkway and make the target individual understand it was just a prank or casual moment, but if mirroring body language elicits positive responses then the two individuals are likely to go ahead and connect.

Lastly, like any other form of communication, the feelings of the target person should be taken into consideration. Even though mirroring of body language is a nonverbal and mostly passive form of nonverbal communication, a human being is an emotional creature, and it is necessary to listen and respond to the feelings of each other. For instance, if the body language of the target person indicates anger, then you should cease or adjust your actions to show consideration and care for the affected person. If the target person that you are mirroring body language is happy, then you should also exhibit positive emotions to increase the shared ground spectrum and encourage the person to exude more positive emotions.

CHAPTER 14

HOW TO USE "MIRRORING" TO IMPROVE YOUR EMPATHY

Mirroring someone else's body language is something we all do automatically, especially if we want to make a connection with them. Smile and the world smile with you are closer to the truth than you might imagine. Have you ever felt happy about something, glad to be alive, and walked through the streets with a smile on your face? Did you notice how many people smiled back at you and maybe initiated a conversation? Smiling, like yawning, is a facial expression we all seem to copy without thinking. We might even start talking like them without realizing.

> *"Similarities help us to form a bond, which is normally reflected in facial expressions and body language"*

Why do we do it?

Some studies have shown that we have a neuron, which controls the recognition of faces, and it is this neuron, which makes us mirror others' expressions. It is a bonding tool and by mirroring others' emotions, it makes the other person feel as if you are empathic and understand how they are feeling.

Even as early as the womb, the baby's heartbeat beats in rhythm with its mother's. As soon as we are born we begin mirroring the facial expressions and body positions we see. If our mother smiles on our faces, we are more likely to smile back. How often have you heard someone say to someone else, "You reminded me of your mother/father?" This is because the mannerisms were the same, copied from an early age. It's how we learn our native tongue and develop a local accent. We are bonded into a group identity, which can be assumed in any situation to integrate us within a new group, or even a new one-on-one relationship or conversation.

Of course, it can also work the other way. A baby or toddler feels validated when his parent mirrors his facial expression. So, the mother might say to the baby, "Are you giving me a smile?" and mirror the action. It is in this way that the child learns what the expression is. Without this skill, the child is less able to relate to others and may not develop the emotion of empathy and so is less like to form well-grounded relationships. This is because that when we form relationships we look for things we have in common with others. Similarities help us to form a bond, which is normally reflected in facial expressions and body language. If this is lacking, then it becomes more difficult to find a rapport with others.

Copycat

If a man does this with a woman, she is likely to think that he is caring and intelligent but don't try and fake it and go overboard because it could end up being farcical. Can you imagine yourself suddenly adopting an Irish accent for instance? Nevertheless, you might subconsciously notice you have a bit of a twang without even trying. However, you might more easily assume the same body position so if she leans forward on the table, you do the same. If she rests her face on her hands, you do it too.

It's also true that if you adopt a particular body position, say standing with your legs apart, you are likely to start experiencing the associated emotion, so you would begin to feel more confident. Crossing the fingers, which is putting the fingertips of each hand together, shows that the person is confident and relaxed. To effect this emotion, assume this position with your hands and the emotion will become real.

Try to become more aware not just of other people's body language and positions but your own because you can control what messages you are sending out to others. Notice if they copy you. If they do, it means that they want to get closer to you and are trying to understand what you are feeling.

Getting the Girl

Of course, this all changes if a man is in the courtship phase with a woman. If a couple is in love it is quite common for them to mirror each other's actions. They will assume the same body language and facial expressions. The closer the couple becomes, the more language is mirrored. Even when you are trying to impress someone who you would like to be closer to, this is a useful tactic to employ. Drink when they drink, smile at the same time and they will believe that you have a lot going on and that you just seem so right together and clicked. Put on some music in the background. The beat of the music should mean that you both start tapping your feet at the same time or move with the same rhythm.

The longer a couple stays together, the more likely they are to start looking like each other. Because they are using the same facial muscles to reflect the other, their muscles start developing similarly. If the mirroring declines over time and turns into a grimace the relationship is more likely to break down. And it will be the one who has more positive facial expressions who is more likely to notice the decline.

Beware of the Situation

Be aware of who you are with when your body starts mimicking theirs. If you are with your boss and your body is doing the same as theirs, they might think you are impertinent or full of yourself. On the other hand, if you are dealing with some jumped up, a pompous fool who thinks that they are better than you go ahead and copy their body language. It will throw them off but be prepared to run too!

Interviews

For instance, if you are going for an interview, quite often interviewers believe they have to adopt a closed, non-committed appearance, which does not reveal their thoughts. They do this so that the interview is not biased towards any candidate and so that everyone receives a fair chance. When you enter the room, be aware that this might be the case and try not to mimic their body language. It will send out the wrong impression. Instead, remember to display open body language. Go in there smiling and make lots of eye contact. If you are convincing, they will begin to adapt your body language and you will know that the interview is going well.

As you gain their confidence and attention, and their body language starts to relax, introduce some mirror images of their body language. If you get them onside you will be able to recognize this, and they will be more likely to help you get what you want: the job, the promotion, the raise.

Crowd Pleasers

It is not unusual for a whole crowd to copy one person's actions. Fans at a concert may leave their seats to stand at the front rather than be the only person sitting. Stadium spectators will start a wave reaction. Studies have been done to show that people will copy others so that they do not stand out in a crowd. For instance, in a waiting room, if one person took a ticket and then threw it away someone watching might assume that they had to do it too. There might be no obvious reason why, but they may sit there and suppose it triggered some mechanism for instance to place them in a queue. When others witnessed this, they followed suit until everyone who entered was taking a ticket from a machine and throwing it away. All for no reason.

If you want to build a strong report, mirroring is a super powerful way to do it and can improve your relationships across the board. Do it to someone you already know well and see what a difference it can make. It is such a strong tool that it might be best to practice before you try for that promotion using it.

CHAPTER 15

HOW TO SPOT INSECURITY

When Someone behaves Irrationally, you have to remind yourself that this could be because they are acting out of a certain emotion, or it also could be that their insecurity is behind this false sense of bravado. When you notice this, you will more likely procure a sense of empathy for these people who act arrogantly or rudely since what they are trying to do is cover their insecurity.

Your ability to spot insecurity can be advantageous to you in several situations. Negotiation, conflict resolution, and even within a problem-solving dynamic. Insecurity can be about anything—looks, power, money, smartness, getting better grades, and so on—and most of these insecurities creep out from a sense of material value Once you do though, it gives you leverage that you can use to connect with the person on a level which they can relate to. In a negotiation situation, this can be extremely useful in swinging the odds into your favor.

> *"Being able to spot insecurity is also going to serve you well in terms of protecting yourself"*

Being able to spot insecurity is also going to serve you well in terms of protecting yourself. Sometimes, these insecure individuals have strong, negative energy about them, and it is easy to get swept up in their emotional turmoil and become insecure yourself if you spend enough time around them. A lack of eye contact, nervous pacing, hunched posture, biting of the fingernails in some cases, repeatedly touching certain parts of the body like the neck, and fidgeting are obvious signs of insecurity and discomfort. Aside from the obvious body language that they display, keep your eyes peeled for the following signs that signal you're dealing with an insecure individual:

- They Make You Feel Insecure Too - Their insecurity will be so strong it starts to rub off on you. You'll want to exercise caution here, since beginning to doubt yourself is going to make you easy prey to manipulators.

- Constant Worry - They're constantly worried that every decision they make is going to reflect badly on them. They express concern about not knowing what the right thing to do is. They ask you what you think several times, or even what you think they should do. They might apologize for being indecisive and unable to decide just yet.

- Showing Off - Insecurity could also manifest itself in a different manner, where the insecure individual feels a constant need to show off their accomplishments just to make themselves feel better. Constantly brag about their amazing lifestyle, their wonderful shoes, their huge cars, and their elite education. All of this is done to convince themselves that they have it all in a poor attempt to feel better about themselves.

- Becoming Defensive - Insecure people become even more nervous, jittery, and on edge when they feel like they are being ganged up on or pressured into deciding. They'll be worried about offending you or making you angry with some of the choices they make, but they may become defensive if they feel like they're being attacked.

- Frequent Complaints - There's always something to complain about when the whole world doesn't seem right to the insecure individual. They'll spend hours, days, weeks, or even months mulling over the concerns and worries, and find it hard to escape that "negative funk" they're in, no matter how much you try to coax them out of it. Even when there's nothing to complain about, they'll be the ones to find something wrong.

- Indecisive Nature - They find it nearly impossible to make a decision and stick to it. They'll second guess, question, bounce from one choice to the next, and keep asking the same question repeatedly, almost as if they're having a hard time accepting the answers they're being given. Even if you gave them a possible solution, they'll reject your initial suggestion, but then come back and circle it again.

Mastering your emotions is essential to dealing with an insecure individual to avoid being easily influenced by their volatile, unpredictable emotional state. Compassion and empathy are especially important, what the insecure person needs are someone who can understand what they're going through. Not someone who is there to judge, criticize, or ridicule. Compassion requires a balanced approach so that our negative emotions are either exaggerated or suppressed when dealing with an insecure individual. This balancing act comes out from the process of relating our personal experiences with that of the suffering of others. Your ability to analyze their body language and read the unspoken communication that goes on is going to be your best asset in a time like this.

Insecurity is an emotional state that arises following a situation that is perceived as alarming or threatening. If the person confronted with this stimulus feels that their resources or skills are insufficient to manage and/or overcome the situation, they are likely to feel insecure. This emotion may manifest itself in the form of higher levels of anxiety, psychomotor agitation, allowing the person to feel unnerved but still able to mobilize extra resources to enable him to succeed. In these cases, insecurity has a protective effect in that it prevents us from making mistakes or taking unnecessary risks. For example, when one of the couples feels that their relationship is not safe, they can implement some strategies that, in their eyes, imply the solidification of the relationship, such as the promotion of dialogue, romantic outings, or even psychotherapeutic follow-up. Similarly, when a worker perceives his or her place as being at risk of being laid off, he or she will seek alternatives to avoid unemployment. But both in one context and the other insecurity can assume a higher level of intensity, no longer having such a protective effect.

These cases, though are likely to be dominated by irrational beliefs, which grow spirally and produce a blocking effect. The person starts to live by what makes him insecure without, however, being able to find adjusted solutions. In the first example, this state of anxiety could translate into a set of behaviors that have both despair and nonsense, such as starting to search the partner's cell for signs of a potential extramarital relationship, aggressive and/or controlling comments, etc. In the following example, it could happen that the person would be so depressed that he would not invest either in the current job or in the search for the new placement, allowing insecurity to have the blocking effect.

What clues or signs are evidenced by someone insecure? How can we identify him?

The most insecure people are overwhelmed by fear, and as a result, it is usually more difficult for them to take an assertive stance, that is, they have very serious difficulties in expressing clearly and honestly what they think and what they feel. Within a group, both can strive to go unnoticed as they can make efforts to please everyone. In practice, they feel an intense fear of failing, of not meeting expectations, of not being up to it. Some people are very confident in professional terms and are more insecure in relational/affective terms. In the same way, some people feel safe and comfortable in the performance of roles related to effective relationships but which reveal serious insecurities in other areas of life. It may not be easy to recognize the most insecure people, especially if the analysis is superficial.

Sometimes it is easier for an insecure individual to recognize another who shares the same insecurities, as he is more aware and more attentive to certain details that will go along with the majority.

Factors Determining Good and Bad

None of these traits helps us to behave virtuously. There is a thin line between being insecure and being a brat. Here are some identifying factors that can help you separate the good and the bad:

1. Self-kindness is not self-judgment.

Compassion towards someone insecure is being understanding and warm to them when they fail, or when we suffer, or at moments when we feel inadequate. We should not be ignoring these emotions or criticizing. People who have compassion understand that being human comes with its imperfections and failing is part of the human experience. There will inevitably be no failure when we attempt something because failure is part of learning and progress.

Things cannot be exactly the way it should be or supposed to be or how we dream it to be. There will be changes and when we accept this with kindness and sympathy and understanding, we experience greater emotional equanimity.

2. Common humanity and not isolation

It is a common human emotion to feel frustrated especially when things do not go the way we envision them to. When this happens, frustration is usually accompanied by irrational isolation, making us feel and think that we are the only person on earth going through this or making dumb mistakes like this. News flash—all humans suffer, all of us go through different kinds of suffering at varying degrees. Compassion involves recognizing that we all suffer and all of us have personal inadequacies. It does not happen to 'Me' or 'I' alone.

3. *Mindfulness is not over-identification.*

Compassion needs us to be balanced with our approach so that our negative emotions are neither exaggerated nor suppressed. This balancing act comes out from the process of relating our personal experiences with that of the suffering of others. This puts the situation we are going through into a larger perspective.

We need to keep mindful awareness so that we can observe our negative thoughts and emotions with clarity and openness. Having a mindful approach is non-judgmental and it is a state of mindful reception that enables us to observe our feelings and thoughts without denying them or suppressing them. There is no way that we can ignore our pain and feel compassion at the same time. By having mindfulness, we also prevent the over-identification of our thoughts and feelings.

Discovering Compassion

You're so dumb! You don't belong here, loser! Those jeans make you look like a fat cow! You can't sit with us! It's safe to say we've all heard some kind of rude, unwanted comments either directly or indirectly aimed at us. Would you talk like this to a friend? Again, the answer is a big NO.

Believe it or not, it is a lot easier and natural for us to be kind and nice to people than to be mean and rude to them whether it is a stranger or someone we care about in our lives. When someone we care about is hurt or is going through a rough time, we console them and say it is ok to fail. We support them when they feel bad about themselves and we comfort them to make them feel better or just to offer a shoulder to cry on.

We are all good at being understanding and compassionate and kind to others. How often do we offer this same kindness and compassion to ourselves? Research on self-compassion shows that those who are compassionate are less likely to be anxious, depressed, or stressed, and more resilient, happy, and optimistic. In other words, they have better mental health.

Identifying Someone with Insecurity

Insecure people tend to spread their negativity and self-doubt to others as well and here is how you can identify them and decide whether to show compassion or to show them the exit:

Insecure people try to make you feel insecure yourself.

You start questioning your ability and self-worth and this happens when you are around a specific person. This individual can manipulate you and talk about their strengths and how they are good in this and that and in a way try to put you down. They project their insecurities on you.

Insecure people need to showcase his or her accomplishments.

Inferiority is at the very core of their behavior and for people like this, compassion to tell them that they are not what they think in their heads is just a waste of your time. They feel insecure and to hide it, talk about their accomplishments, not in a good way but constantly brag about their amazing lifestyle, their wonderful shoes, their huge cars, and their elite education. All this is done to convince themselves that they do have it all and you have none.

People who are insecure drops the "humblebrag" far too much.

The humblebrag is essentially a brag that is disguised as a self-derogatory statement. In this social media age, you can see plenty of humblebrags who complain about their first-world problems such as all the travel they need to do or the amount of time they spend watching their kids play and win games or even the person who complains about having a tiny pimple when the rest of their face looks flawless. Social media is ripe with narcissistic people, and this is not worth your time. Do not feel any less just because someone shows off how much traveling they need to do.

Insecure people frequently complain that things aren't good enough.

They like showing off the high standards that they have, and while you may label them as snobs, it might be a harder feeling to shake off because you might be thinking that they are better than you although you know that it is all an act. They proclaim their high standards to assert that they are doing better than everyone else and make you feel less of yourself and more miserable. Pay no attention to people like this.

How to Spot a Dangerous Person

There are always people at the extremes of each trait and, sometimes, these people can be dangerous. While most people exhibit a fair few 'good' personality traits, and perhaps a couple of 'bad' ones, some people exhibit a singular bad trait so strongly or even several bad traits at a low level. Such people can be anything from mildly annoying, lacking in social skills, to downright manipulative or abusive. Most concerning is the fact that some people can mask these negative traits quite well. How many times have you met someone you thought was friendly enough, only to realize later that they are not someone you want to know at all? What about friends you have who act one way in one situation but can be completely different at other times? Everyone would do well to remember that no matter how good we get at analyzing and speed-reading others, there is always a chance that something important will escape our notice, or that the other person will be able to mask their intentions too well.

Despite this, there are some red flags for which we can learn to watch out. These apply to all of our relationships – not just romantic ones. Identifying personality types that may do us harm involves understanding what healthy relationships look like, whether they are with family members, friends, colleagues, superiors, and yes, romantic or sexual partners. Here is a list of some telltale signs that something's wrong in your interaction with another person. Their behavior points to their personality – and if their personality is harming you, then you are always within your rights to step back, get out, and look for support to ensure your safety, physically, emotionally, and mentally. Identifying one of these red flags in your relationship with someone doesn't mean you have to cut ties with them immediately, but it should give you pause about how you'd like things to change in the future.

CHAPTER 16

HOW TO SHOW DOMINANCE THROUGH BODY LANGUAGE

People who want to imply being in charge usually use dominant nonverbal cues. These people may not be aware of these body language signals may not even be aware that they are doing so and may just be a factor in their dominant personality.

Used properly, showing dominance through body language can help you gain respect and popularity, a method usually employed by politicians during the campaign period. Here are some actions that express dominance.

> *"Body language can be used to show dominance and influence the action of others"*

Appearing Larger

Appearing larger and more powerful is an important factor in showing dominance, and this can be traced back to man's prehistoric roots. This action is also very evident in animals, where fights for dominance are often settled by size comparison, saving the parties involved from altercations.

This behavioral bias was inherited by modern humans and can be seen practiced when competing with others. Using the same size and body language signal, they try to show their superiority by appearing to be threatening and should be avoided. Here are examples of these size signals:

Make Your Body Appear Bigger

A bigger person is often seen as more dominant and more threatening. If you have the height advantage, then good for you because you are already large, and this effect comes naturally to you. It's one of the main reasons why taller people tend to be more successful than others, not only in sports but also in the corporate world. For the smaller ones, here are some gestures, postures, and body language tricks to appear bigger.

Place your hand on your hips. This will make you appear wider than you usually are, thus adding to your size.

Stand upright. Straightening your back can add inches to your height.

Sit or stand with your legs apart. This applies to men, and like placing your hands on your hips, it also adds to your 'width.'

Hold your head and chin up. Another technique you can use to add to your height.

Stand Higher

When you are standing higher than the other person, you are in a more dominant position giving you a natural advantage. You can do this by:

Stand while the other party sits. This instantly gives you the height advantage.

Stand on a platform or step to give you extra height when compared with the other party

Stand tall and straight. Tiptoe if you must.

Wear a large hat or wear high heel shoes.

Style your hair to make you look taller. This is common practice with women.

Remember, people who make themselves appear larger or bigger aim to be more dominant, threatening, or powerful.

Claiming Territory

Humans are quite territorial, thanks to our ancestral origins and heritage. People shot a lot of territorial signals, and you can use these to predict behavior. When trying to be more dominant, you can do the following nonverbal signals to claim territory:

Claim a particular area in a conference room, exhibition center, meeting room, or office room and expect other people to comply with the rules you set for that area.

Invade the personal space of the other person to imply dominance. You can even emphasize the act with a touch like lightly holding the arm or patting the person's back, which indicates ownership. A study showed that a show of affection may not always be the reason when a man touches a woman. Instead, it can be a show of dominance or ownership.

Invade an area currently owned by the other person. You can sit at the edge of that person's table or on their chair, which is a common gesture of dominance. This move is often used by power-tripping managers or bosses who invade other people's territory to show them who is in charge.

Touch or hold the other person's possessions. When this gesture is made with a relaxed composure, this implies that you own what they own, which is another indication of domination. You may pick the other person's favorite pen or phone or rearrange their desk. It's like saying, 'what's yours is also mine, and you can't do anything to stop me.'

Walk in the center of the corridor so that other people stay out of your way. This is a claim to a common territory, which implies authority and dominance over others. The same can be observed from some drivers during heavy traffic wherein they don't let other drivers merge into their lane.

When the meeting room has a long table, sit at one end. This position is usually reserved for someone with a superior role or power. Sitting here emphasizes your dominance over others.

When talking with a group, position yourself at the center, which forces others to pay attention to what you're discussing. Since your back will be vulnerable, ensure that the persons you trust are behind you.

Signaling Superiority

There are various direct or indirect power cues that you can show if you want to appear dominant, particularly in social contexts. You can either plan these signals or improvise when the need arises. These power signals can be a combination of verbal and nonverbal languages. Here are some of the techniques that you can use:

Show of Dominance through Wealth

Wear expensive clothes, watch, jewelry, accessories, and makeup. Doing so makes you appear rich, powerful, and well-connected.

Show off your possessions indirectly. This can be done by paying hefty bills in a relaxed manner, flashing the latest flagship mobile phone, or driving an expensive car.

Show of Dominance through Control

Order a staff or team member to bring you something in front of another person. This implies that you are in charge of the area. For example, you can tell someone to bring you a cup of coffee, print a certain report immediately, or have them call another person and bring that person into the meeting room.

Controlling and giving orders can also be combined with a display of wealth to emphasize its importance. For example, call your secretary while in the presence of others and have her book you a business class flight, a five-star hotel with all the bells and whistles, and a chauffeured luxury car. Showing that you can get whatever you want indicates power and dominance, and this is a move usually exhibited by top corporate executives to impress their customers.

Controlling Time

No, you don't need a time machine for this technique. Similar to dominating other people's space, you can control their time as well by setting a pace for them to follow. You can use nonverbal cues to exert time pressure on other people. Here are some verbal and nonverbal techniques you can use:

Interrupt

Interrupt a discussion by leaving early or arriving late

Hurry Other People

Set a fast pace for other people to follow

Walk using wide strides. This implies you're determined a certain goal quickly and that you are confident with your actions. When you're walking with another person, walk a bit faster to set your own pace. This shows who's in charge, and the slower person will be forced to also walk fast to keep up.

Talk faster than usual. This forces others to also talk fast and give you control of their time.

Slow Down Other People

When talking with another person, interrupt him by asking for a concise and brief talk. This implies you value your time more than his. You can also use this technique when breaking a pace set by another person so you can change the discussion's focus. This may also be effective in counteracting the hurried pace of a dominant person.

Facial Expressions

To show dominance, it's important to extensively use facial expressions to show power and control. Here are some examples.

Avoid Eye Contact

To suggest that someone is not important to you, you can simply avoid looking at them.

Make Prolonged Eye Contact

When you gaze at the other person intensely while proving a point, it implies that you stand by your word, and you're not budging an inch.

It also shows dominance, being uncooperative and unwilling, and being strong-minded.

Make a Neutral Face

This can be very useful during negotiations because making this facial expression can be interpreted by the other person that you are unimpressed. When you hold this facial expression while another person is pitching his product or case enthusiastically, it can cause him to buckle or be unnerved. This is often exhibited during academic debates when a domain or subject expert, such as a professor, wants to show dominance by showing that he's not interested in the other person's ideas.

Smile Sparingly

People who want to show dominance smile less often than the submissive ones. Although there's a chance that some people might dislike you, smiling less often shows you mean business and you are in control.

Display Your Crotch (Applies Only to Men)

Of course, you need to have your pants on when you do this move or risk spending the night inside the jail. Stand with your feet shoulder-width apart with both feet firmly planted on the ground. This is called standing crotch display and is a very masculine way of highlighting your genitals to show dominance or superiority. You can emphasize this move by 'adjusting' or lightly 'touching' the crotch area. You can also do this technique by sitting down by opening your legs and knees.

It's very uncommon for women to show this gesture because it can be interpreted as an invitation to sexual intimacy, although some may do so as a show of strength and equality with men.

Counteract Dominance

But what if another person in the room is showing dominance using the techniques mentioned above? You can derail their actions by utilizing these nonverbal strategies:

Return the Gaze

If the other person looks you in the eye longer than what you consider normal, look back, and return the gaze. Doing so might get you distracted by their piercing eyes, but there's a way around that. Instead of looking directly into their eyes, imagine a triangle formed by the eyes and forehead and then look at the center of that triangle.

Initiate the First Touch

Just before that person is about to touch you, touch him first. Or retaliate with your touch when he touched you. This shows that you're not one to mess with or dominate.

Take it Slow

When the dominant person is trying to rush you, breathe slowly, remain calm, and slow down the pace. This can imply that there's no need to hurry. Show that the slower pace you're trying to set is more ideal and be persistent about it. This applies to both walking and talking

Use Humor

A dominant person always aims to take over conversations. Break that dominance by telling a joke and take back control of the conversation. You can get a laugh by telling a joke or using nonverbal actions. You can use this break to shift the discussion back to your preferred topic.

Body language can be used to show dominance and influence the action of others. You can also use it to counteract imposed dominance by others.

CONCLUSION

Everything that a person does or says reveals something about their personality. Actions, beliefs, and thoughts of people are aligned perfectly with each other in a way that they all reveal the same things concerning an individual. Just as it is said that all methods can lead to Rome, everything a person thinks or does can reveal a lot about their personality makeup and personality. Words that are spoken by a person, even if they carry less weight, tell a great deal about a person's insecurities and desires.

No one doubts that the words we speak or write are a full expression of our inner personalities and thoughts. However, beyond the real content of a language, exclusive insights into the minds of the author are usually hidden in the text's style.

From our acts of dominance to truthfulness, we are revealing to others too much about us. You can quickly know the most important of all the people in the room by listening to the words that they use. Confident and high-status people use very few "I" words. The higher a person's status is in a given situation, the less the "I" words they will use in their conversations.

Each time people feel confident, they tend to focus on the task that they have at hand, and not necessarily on them. "I" is also used less in the weeks that follow a given cultural upheaval. As age kicks on, we tend to use more positive emotional words and even make very fewer references to ourselves.

It is important to be true to yourself. The tips and techniques discussed in this book are not to help you become someone else. Quite the contrary. I have intended to help you let your true self shine. Regardless of what your personality is like, these tips and strategies will help you let your personality shine. People will seek you for who you are. In a dating context, anyone interested in you will do so because they can see that you are authentic and relatable. As I stated earlier, if you pretend to be someone you are not, this will eventually backfire on you.

Goood luck

Jason

Printed in Great Britain
by Amazon